Dedication

This Book is dedicated to the Almighty God.

ACKNOWLEDGEMENT

A book such as this result from the collaborative effort of several individuals too numerous to mention.

However, the first among those who saw me through the establishment of this book is unquestionably my parents, Mr. & Mrs. Friday Akenuwa who supported me financially. Their care and support as catapulted me from Zero to Hero.   Next is my youth leader, Mst Henry Nwabueze, who through pain made research and provided key points. His encouragement, especially when our zeal began to flag was perhaps the major reason why this book became a reality.   Not forgetting my brothers and sisters who's support and encouragement has brought me thus far.

Finally, ı must extend my gratitude to all the people, whose contributions have found their way into this book "His the United State still the land of the free and home to the brave?". In virtually every aspect, they have provided useful and sometimes controversial insight into complex subjects and concepts.

Preface

A book such as this was written because of the things going on in the United States of America. "His the United States still the land of the free and home to the brave" is all about American in general, the police brutality going on, hate among the citizens, racism, lies and lot more.

It was important that this book come out at this point in time when so many wants to migrate to the States to seek for a greener pasture, just to let the know that America though promises good life, it also causes pain and emotional worries to foreigner especially the black race. It also to bring to the eyes of the world how cowardly American politician tends to treat the race issue currently affecting the American people.

On my journey to writing this book, I have faced so many challenges and criticism, from all works and life, I have even faced a life threatened situation all just to make me change my mind and not exposed the wrong doings of the American States. But in all that pressure, I was determined to never give up.

It took me 2 years to put together Ideals and researched I have collected on the path to writing this book and all the ideal given to me by various works of life is what as help me thus far to be confident and bring out a book such as this.

INTRODUCTION

Back when we were little, if you asked us then what we wanted to be when we grew up, we would likely have responded, with a sheepish grin, "Pilot" or "Soldier" or "Musician". Becoming an entrepreneur with half-dozen diverse businesses, much less a motivational writer would never have crossed our mind.

Becoming an author of book and show casing my ability to put ideals to writing was outside my imagination as well.

My father, a soldier and successful Federal Government Worker hoped that I would become a preacher. My mother, an entrepreneur and a teacher in her own right, probably though that I would become a pilot. None of us envisioned me ministering to thousands of people through my writing.

My life has constantly changed as I respond to events, people, and opportunities.

I've also made deliberate attempts to grow, to position myself to receive, and to reposition myself to receive more.

I have failed and tried again, many time, before making significant progress toward my goals. I gained experience and did not allow my past failure to bind and gag me.

The boundaries established in my own mind for how far I could go were pushed outward. I found the keys to living without limits.

Many of us attribute success or failure to fate or some external force. We believe that we have to be in the right place at the right time in order to achieve, much like winning the lottery. But success is a direct consequence of our wanting a more abundant life and working hard to earn it, like wading through the mud puddles of life toward the beckoning sea.

Too many people think freedom can be attributed to just speech, movement, worship and lot more. But so many people don't have the ideal that their free right have been taken away from then.

Too often the term freedom gets hijacked to mean nothing more than an elusive state of temporary bliss and positive karma.

His the United State still the land of the free and home to the brave? : Rediscovering the lost glory and help to speak the truth of what is going on in America as a whole.

As you read through this book with raped attention and get determine to be among the change that is to begin in America, then you will discover that you just gave the next generation the reason to live.

Remain blessed.

Table of contents

IS THE UNITED STATES STILL THE LAND OF THE FREE AND HOME TO THE BRAVE?

This is a great question the world needs to ask. But before I go further to explain why I think the United States is no longer the land of the free and home to the brave, let me say little about how the United States came to be.

The United States of America (USA), commonly referred to as the United States (U.S.) or America, is a federal republic consisting of 50 states and a federal district. The 48 contiguous states and Washington, D.C., are in central North America between Canada and Mexico. The state of Alaska is located in the northwestern part of North America and the state of Hawaii is an archipelago in the mid-Pacific. The country also has five populated and nine unpopulated territories in the Pacific and the Caribbean. At 3.80 million square miles (9.85 million km²) and with over 320 million people, the United States is the world's fourth-largest country by total area and third most populous. It is one of the world's most ethnically diverse and multicultural nations, the product of large-scale immigration from many countries. The geography and climate of the United States are also extremely diverse, and the country is home to a wide variety of wildlife.

Paleo-Indians migrated from Eurasia to what is now the U.S. mainland around 15,000 years ago, with European colonization beginning in the 16th century. The United States emerged from 13 British colonies located along the East Coast. Disputes between Great Britain and the colonies led to the American Revolution. On July 4, 1776, as the colonies were fighting Great Britain in the American Revolutionary War, delegates from the 13 colonies unanimously adopted the Declaration of Independence. The war ended in 1783 with recognition of the independence of the United States by the Kingdom of Great Britain, and was the first successful war of independence against a European colonial empire. The country's constitution was adopted on September 17, 1787 and ratified by the states in 1788. The first ten amendments, collectively named the Bill of Rights, were ratified in 1791 and designed to guarantee many fundamental civil rights and freedoms.

Driven by the doctrine of Manifest Destiny, the United States embarked on a vigorous expansion across North America throughout the 19th century. This involved displacing American Indian tribes, acquiring new territories, and gradually admitting new states, until by 1848 the nation spanned the continent. During the second half of the 19th century, the American Civil War ended legal slavery in the country. By the end of that century, the United States extended into the Pacific Ocean, and the economy, driven in large part by the Industrial Revolution, began to soar.The Spanish–American War and World War I confirmed the country's status as a global military power. The United States emerged from World War II as a global superpower, the first country to develop nuclear weapons, the only country to use them in warfare, and as a permanent member of the United Nations Security Council. The end of the Cold War and the dissolution of the Soviet Union left the United States as the sole superpower.

The United States is a developed country and has the world's largest national economy, benefiting from an abundance of natural resources and high worker productivity. While the U.S. economy is considered post-industrial, the country continues to be one of the world's largest manufacturers. Accounting for 37% of global military spending and 19% of world GDP (PPP), it isthe world's foremost economic and military power, a prominent political and cultural force, and a leader in scientific research and technological innovations.

Etymology

In 1507, the German cartographer Martin Waldseemuller produced a world map on which he named the lands of the Western Hemisphere "America" after the Italian explorer and cartographer Amerigo Vespucci (Latin: *Americus Vespucius*). The first documentary evidence of the phrase "United States of America" is from a letter dated January 2, 1776, written by Stephen Moylan, Esq.,George Washington's aide-de-camp and Muster-Master General of the Continental Army. Addressed to Lt. Col. Joseph Reed, Moylan expressed his wish to carry the "full and ample powers of the United States of America" to Spain to assist in the revolutionary war effort.

The first known publication of the phrase "United States of America" was in an anonymously written essay in *The Virginia Gazette*newspaper in Williamsburg, Virginia, on April 6, 1776. In June 1776, Thomas Jefferson included the phrase "UNITED STATES OF AMERICA" in all capitalized letters in the headline of his "original Rough draught" of the Declaration of Independence. In the finalFourth of

July version of the Declaration, the pertinent section of the title was changed to read, "The unanimous Declaration of the thirteen united States of America". In 1777 the Articles of Confederation announced, "The Stile of this Confederacy shall be 'The United States of America'".

The short form "United States" is also standard. Other common forms include the "U.S.", the "USA", and "America". Colloquial names include the "U.S. of A." and, internationally, the "States". "Columbia", a name popular in poetry and songs of the late 1700s, derives its origin from Christopher Columbus; it appears in the name "District of Columbia". In non-English languages, the name is frequently the translation of either the "United States" or "United States of America", and colloquially as "America". In addition, an abbreviation (e.g. USA) is sometimes used.

The phrase "United States" was originally treated as plural, a description of a collection of independent states—e.g., "the United States are"—including in the Thirteenth Amendment to the United States Constitution, ratified in 1865. It became common to treat it as singular, a single unit—e.g., "the United States is"—after the end of the Civil War. The singular form is now standard; the plural form is retained in the idiom "these United States". The difference has been described as more significant than one of usage, but reflecting the difference between a collection of states and a unit.

The standard way to refer to a citizen of the United States is as an "American". "United States", "American" and "U.S." are used to refer to the country adjectivally ("American values", "U.S. forces"). "American" is rarely used in English to refer to subjects not connected with the United States.

History of the United States

Part of a series on the

History of the United States

When to date the start of the **history of the United States** is debated among historians. Older textbooks start with the arrival of Christopher Columbus in 1492 and emphasize the European background, or they start in 1600 and emphasize the American frontier. In recent decades American schools and universities typically have shifted back in time to include more on the colonial period and much more on the prehistory of the Native peoples.

Indigenous peoples lived in what is now the United States for thousands of years and developed complex cultures before European colonists began to arrive, mostly from England, after 1600. The Spanish had small settlements in Florida and the Southwest, and the French along the Mississippi River and the Gulf Coast. By the 1770s, thirteen British colonies contained two and a half million people along the Atlantic coast east of the Appalachian Mountains. In the 1760s the British government imposed a series of new taxes while rejecting the American argument that any new taxes had to be approved by the people. Tax resistance, especially the Boston Tea Party(1774), led to punitive laws (the Intolerable Acts) by Parliament designed to end self-government in Massachusetts. American Patriots (as they were called at the time as a term of ridicule) adhered to a political ideology called republicanism that emphasized civic duty, virtue, and opposition to corruption, fancy luxuries and aristocracy.

All thirteen colonies united in a Congress that called on the colonies to write new state constitutions. After armed conflict began in Massachusetts, Patriots drove the royal officials out of every colony and assembled in mass meetings and conventions. Those Patriot governments in the colonies unanimously empowered their delegates to Congress to declare independence. In 1776, Congress created an independent nation, the United States of America. With large-scale military and financial support from France and military leadership by General George Washington, the American Patriots won the Revolutionary War. The peace treaty of 1783 gave the new nation the land east of the Mississippi River (except Florida and Canada). The central government established by the Articles of Confederation proved ineffectual at providing stability, as it had no authority to collect taxes and had no executive officer. Congress called a convention to meet secretly in Philadelphia in 1787 to revise the Articles of Confederation. It wrote a new Constitution, which was adopted in 1789. In 1791, a Bill of Rights was added to guarantee inalienable rights. With Washington as the Union's first president and Alexander Hamilton his chief political and financial adviser, a strong central government was created. When Thomas Jefferson became president he purchased the Louisiana Territory from France, doubling the size of the United States. A second and last war with Britain was fought in 1812.

Encouraged by the notion of Manifest Destiny, federal territory expanded all the way to the Pacific. The expansion was driven by a quest for inexpensive land for yeoman farmers and slave owners. The expansion of slavery was increasingly controversial and fueled political and constitutional battles, which were resolved by compromises. Slavery was abolished in all states north of the Mason–Dixon line by 1804, but the South continued to profit off the institution, producing high-value cotton exports to feed increasing high demand in Europe. The 1860 presidential election of Republican Abraham Lincoln was on a platform of ending the expansion of slavery and putting it on a path to extinction. Seven cotton-based deep South slave states seceded and later founded the Confederacy months before Lincoln's inauguration. No nation ever recognized the Confederacy, but it opened the war by attacking Fort Sumter in 1861. A surge of nationalist outrage in the North fueled a long, intense American Civil War (1861-1865). It was fought largely in the South as the overwhelming material and manpower advantages of the North proved decisive in a long war. The war's result was restoration of the Union, the impoverishment of the South, and the abolition of slavery. In the Reconstruction era (1863–1877), legal and voting rights were extended to the freed slave. The national government emerged much stronger, and because of the Fourteenth Amendment, it gained the explicit duty to protect individual rights. However, when white Democrats regained their power in the South during the 1870s, often by paramilitary suppression of voting, they passed Jim Crow laws to maintain white supremacy, and new disfranchising constitutions that prevented most African Americans and many poor whites from voting, a situation that continued for decades until gains of the civil rights movement in the 1960s and passage of federal legislation to enforce constitutional rights.

The United States became the world's leading industrial power at the turn of the 20th century due to an outburst of entrepreneurship in the Northeast and Midwest and the arrival of millions of immigrant workers and farmers from Europe. The national railroad network was completed with the work of Chinese immigrants and large-scale mining and factories industrialized the Northeast and Midwest. Mass dissatisfaction with corruption, inefficiency and traditional politics stimulated the Progressive movement, from the 1890s to 1920s, which led to many social and political reforms. In 1920, the 19th Amendment to the Constitution guaranteed women's suffrage (right to vote). This followed the 16th and 17th amendments in 1913, which established the first national income tax and direct election of US senators to Congress. Initially neutral during World War

I, the US declared war on Germany in 1917 and later funded the Allied victory the following year. After a prosperous decade in the 1920s, the Wall Street Crash of 1929 marked the onset of the decade-long world-wide Great Depression. Democratic President Franklin D. Roosevelt ended the Republican dominance of the White House and implemented his New Deal programs for relief, recovery, and reform. The New Deal, which defined modern American liberalism, included relief for the unemployed, support for farmers, Social Security and a minimum wage. After the Japanese attack on Pearl Harbor on December 7, 1941, the United States later entered World War II along with Britain, the Soviet Union, and the smaller Allies. The U.S. financed the Allied war effort and helped defeat Nazi Germany in Europe and defeated Imperial Japan in the Pacific War by detonating newly invented atomic bombs on enemy targets.

The United States and the Soviet Union emerged as rival superpowers after World War II. During the Cold War, the US and the USSR confronted each other indirectly in the arms race, the Space Race, proxy wars, and propaganda campaigns. US foreign policy during the Cold War was built around the support of Western Europe and Japan along with the policy of "containment" or stopping the spread of communism. The US joined the wars in Korea and Vietnam to try to stop its spread. In the 1960s, in large part due to the strength of the civil rights movement, another wave of social reforms were enacted by enforcing the constitutional rights of voting and freedom of movement to African-Americans and other racial minorities. Native American activism also rose. The Cold War ended when the Soviet Union officially dissolved in 1991, leaving the United States as the world's only superpower. As the 21st century began, international conflict centered around the Middle East following the September 11 attacks by Al-Qaeda on the United States in 2001. In 2008, the United States had its worst economic crisis since the Great Depression, which has been followed by slower than usual rates of economic growth during the 2010s.

Pre-Columbian era

Prehistory of the United States and *Pre-Columbian era*

It is not definitively known how or when the Native Americans first settled the Americas and the present-day United States. The prevailing theory proposes that people migrated from Eurasia across Beringia, a land bridge that connected Siberia to present-day Alaska during the Ice Age, and then spread southward throughout the Americas and possibly going as far south as the Antarctic peninsula. This migration may have begun as early as 30,000 years ago[3] and continued through to about 10,000+ years ago, when the land bridge became submerged by the rising sea level caused by the ending of the last glacial period.[4] These early inhabitants, called Paleoamericans, soon diversified into many hundreds of culturally distinct nations and tribes.

The pre-Columbian era incorporates all [period subdivisions](#) in the [history and prehistory of the Americas](#) before the appearance of significant European influences on the [American](#)continents, spanning the time of the [original settlement](#) in the [Upper Paleolithic](#) period to [European colonization](#) during the [Early Modern period](#). While technically referring to the era before [Christopher Columbus](#)' voyages of 1492 to 1504, in practice the term usually includes the history of [American indigenous cultures](#) until they were conquered or significantly influenced by Europeans, even if this happened decades or even centuries after Columbus' initial landing.

Colonial period

The Spanish [conquistador](#)[Coronado](#) explored parts of the[American Southwest](#) from 1540 to 1542.

[Colonial history of the United States](#)

After a [period of exploration sponsored by major European nations](#), the first successful English settlement was established in 1607. Europeans brought horses, cattle, and hogs to the Americas and, in turn, took back to Europe maize, [turkeys](#), potatoes, tobacco, beans, and [squash](#). Many explorers and early settlers died after being exposed to new diseases in the Americas. The effects of new Eurasian diseases carried by the colonists, especially smallpox and measles, were much worse for the Native Americans, as they had no [immunity](#) to them. They [suffered epidemics](#) and died in very large numbers, usually before large-scale European settlement began. Their societies were disrupted and hollowed out by the scale of deaths.

Spanish, Dutch, and French colonization

Juan Ponce de León (Santervás de Campos, Valladolid, Spain). He was one of the first Europeans to arrive to the current U.S. because led the first European expedition to Florida, which he named.

Main articles: Spanish colonization of the Americas, Dutch colonization of the Americas and French colonization of the Americas

Spanish explorers were the first Europeans with Christopher Columbus' second expedition, to reach Puerto Rico on November 19, 1493; others reached Florida in 1513.Spanish expeditions quickly reached the Appalachian Mountains, the Mississippi River, the Grand Canyon and theGreat Plains. In 1540, Hernando de Soto undertook an extensive exploration of the Southeast. That same year, Francisco Vásquez de Coronadoexplored from Arizona to central Kansas. Small Spanish settlements eventually grew to become important cities, such as San Antonio, Texas,Albuquerque, New Mexico, Tucson, Arizona, Los Angeles, California, and San Francisco, California.

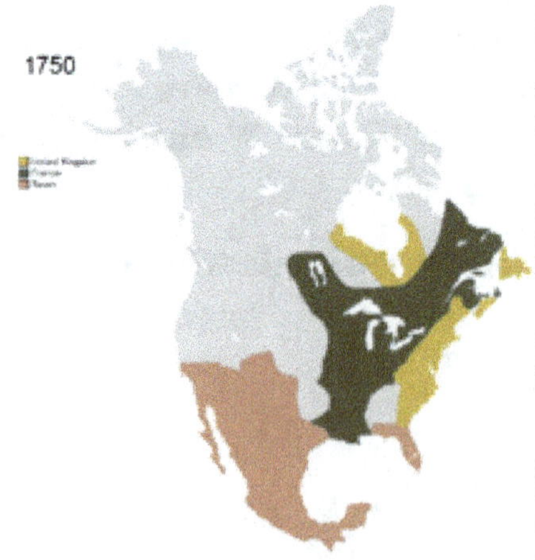

European territorial claims in North America, c. 1750

New Netherland was a 17th-century Dutch colony centered on present-day New York City and the Hudson River Valley; the Dutch traded furs with the Native Americans to the north. The colony served as a barrier to expansion from New England. Despite being Calvinists and building the Reformed Church in America, the Dutch were tolerant of other religions and cultures. The colony, which was taken over by Britain in 1664, left an enduring legacy on American cultural and political life; this includes secular broad-mindedness and mercantile pragmatism in the city as well as rural traditionalism in the countryside (typified by the story of Rip Van Winkle). Notable Americans of Dutch descent include Martin Van Buren, Theodore Roosevelt, Franklin D. Roosevelt, Eleanor Roosevelt and the Frelinghuysens.

New France was the area colonized by France from 1534 to 1763. There were few permanent settlers outside Quebec and Acadia, but the French had far-reaching trading relationships with Native Americans throughout the Great Lakes and Midwest. French villages along the Mississippi and Illinois rivers were based in farming communities that served as a granary for Gulf Coast settlements. The French established plantations in Louisiana along with settling New Orleans, Mobile and Biloxi.

The WabanakiConfederacy were military allies of New France through the four French and Indian Wars while the British colonies were allied with the Iroquois Confederacy. During the French and Indian War – the North American theater of theSeven Years' War – New England fought successfully against French Acadia. The British removed Acadians from Acadia (Nova Scotia) and replaced them with New England Planters. Eventually, some Acadians resettled in Louisiana, where they developed a distinctive rural Cajunculture that still exists. They became American citizens in 1803 with the Louisiana Purchase. Other French villages along the Mississippi and Illinois rivers were absorbed when the Americans started arriving after 1770, or settlers moved west to escape them. French influence and language in New Orleans, Louisiana and the Gulf Coast was more enduring; New Orleans was notable for its large population of free people of color before the Civil War.

British colonization

Further information: British colonization of the Americas

The *Mayflower*, which transported Pilgrims to the New World. During the first winter at Plymouth, about half of the Pilgrims died.

The strip of land along the eastern seacoast was settled primarily by English colonists in the 17th century along with much smaller numbers of Dutch and Swedes. Colonial America was defined by a severe labor shortage that employed forms of unfree labor such as slavery and indentured servitude and by a British policy of benign neglect (salutary neglect). Over half of all European immigrants to Colonial America arrived as indentured servants. Salutary neglect permitted the development of an American spirit distinct from that of its European founders.

The first successful English colony, Jamestown, was established in 1607 on the James River in Virginia. Jamestown languished for decades until a new wave of settlers arrived in the late 17th century and established commercial agriculture based on tobacco. Between the late 1610s and the Revolution, the British shipped an estimated 50,000 convicts to their American colonies. A severe instance of conflict was the 1622 Powhatan uprising in Virginia in which Native Americans killed hundreds of English settlers. The largest conflicts between Native Americans and English settlers in the 17th century were King Philip's War in New England and the Yamasee War in South Carolina.

The massacre of Jamestown settlers in 1622. Soon the colonists in the South feared all natives as enemies.

New England was initially settled primarily by Puritans. The Pilgrims established a settlement in 1620 at Plymouth Colony, which was followed by the establishment of the Massachusetts Bay Colony in 1630. The Middle Colonies, consisting of the present-day states of New York, New Jersey, Pennsylvania, and Delaware, were characterized by a large degree of diversity. The first attempted English settlement south of Virginia was the Province of Carolina, with Georgia Colony – the last of the Thirteen Colonies – established in 1733.

The colonies were characterized by religious diversity, with many Congregationalists in New England, German and Dutch Reformed in the Middle Colonies, Catholics in Maryland, and Scots-Irish Presbyterians on the frontier. Sephardic Jews were among early settlers in cities of New England and the South. Many immigrants arrived as religious refugees: French Huguenots settled in New York, Virginia and the Carolinas. Many royal officials and merchants were Anglicans.

Religiosity expanded greatly after the First Great Awakening, a religious revival in the 1740s led by preachers such as Jonathan Edwards and George Whitefield. American Evangelicals affected by the Awakening added a new emphasis on divine outpourings of the Holy Spirit and conversions that implanted within new believers an intense love for God. Revivals encapsulated those hallmarks and carried the newly created evangelicalism into the early republic, setting the stage for the Second Great Awakening beginning in the late 1790s. In the early stages, evangelicals in the South such as Methodists and Baptists preached for religious freedom and abolition of slavery; they converted many slaves and recognized some as preachers.

Each of the 13 American colonies had a slightly different governmental structure. Typically, a colony was ruled by a governor appointed from London who controlled the executive administration and relied upon a locally elected legislature to vote taxes and make laws. By the 18th century, the American colonies were growing very rapidly as a result of low death rates along with ample supplies of land and food. The colonies were richer than most parts of Britain, and attracted a steady flow of immigrants, especially teenagers who arrived as indentured servants. The tobacco and rice plantations imported African slaves for labor from the British colonies in the West Indies, and by the 1770s African slaves comprised a fifth of the American population. The question of independence from Britain did not arise as long as the colonies needed British military support against the French and Spanish powers; those threats were gone by 1765. London regarded the American colonies as existing for the benefit of the mother country. This policy is known as mercantilism.

18th century

Political integration and autonomy

[Join, or Die](#): This 1756 political cartoon by **[Benjamin Franklin](#)** urged the colonies to join together during the French and Indian War.

The **[French and Indian War](#)** (1754–63) was a watershed event in the political development of the colonies. It was also part of the larger **[Seven Years' War](#)**. The influence of the main rivals of the British Crown in the colonies and Canada, the French and North American Indians, was significantly reduced with the territory of the **[Thirteen Colonies](#)** expanding into **[New France](#)** both in Canada and the **[Louisiana Territory](#)**. Moreover, the war effort resulted in greater political integration of the colonies, as reflected in the **[Albany Congress](#)** and symbolized by**[Benjamin Franklin](#)**'s call for the colonies to "Join or Die". Franklin was a man of many inventions – one of which was the concept of a United States of America, which emerged after 1765 and was realized in July 1776.

Following Britain's acquisition of French territory in North America, **[King George III](#)** issued the **[Royal Proclamation of 1763](#)** with the goal of organizing the new North American empire and protecting the native Indians from colonial expansion into western lands beyond the Appalachian Mountains. In ensuing years, strains developed in the relations between the colonists and the Crown. The **[British Parliament](#)**passed the **[Stamp Act of 1765](#)**, imposing a tax on the colonies without going through the colonial legislatures. The issue was drawn: did Parliament have this right to tax Americans who were not represented in it? Crying "**[No taxation without representation](#)**", the colonists refused to pay the taxes as tensions escalated in the late 1760s and early 1770s.

1846 painting of the 1773 **[Boston Tea Party](#)**.

The **[Boston Tea Party](#)** in 1773 was a direct action by activists in the town of Boston to protest against the new tax on tea. Parliament quickly responded the next year with the Coercive Acts, stripping Massachusetts of its historic right of self-government and putting it under army rule, which sparked outrage and resistance in all thirteen colonies. Patriot leaders from all 13 colonies convened the First Continental Congress to coordinate their resistance to the Coercive Acts. The Congress called for a boycott of British trade, published a list of rights and grievances, andpetitioned the king for redress of those grievances. The appeal to the Crown had no effect, and so the Second Continental Congress was convened in 1775 to organize the defense of the colonies against the British Army.

Ordinary folk became insurgents against the British even though they were unfamiliar with the ideological rationales being offered. They held very strongly a sense of "rights" that they felt the British were deliberately violating – rights that stressed local autonomy, fair dealing, and government by consent. They were highly sensitive to the issue of tyranny, which they saw manifested in the arrival in Boston of the British Army to punish the Bostonians. This heightened their sense of violated rights, leading to rage and demands for revenge. They had faith that God was on their side.

The American Revolutionary War began at Concord and Lexington in April 1775 when the British tried to seize ammunition supplies and arrest the Patriot leaders.

Population density in the American Colonies in 1775.

In terms of political values, the Americans were largely united on a concept called Republicanism, that rejected aristocracy and emphasized civic duty and a fear of corruption. For the Founding Fathers, according to one team of historians, "republicanism represented more than a particular form of government. It was a way of life, a core ideology, an uncompromising commitment to liberty, and a total rejection of aristocracy."

American Revolution

[American Revolution](#) and *[History of the United States (1776–89)](#)*

[Washington's surprise crossing of the Delaware River](#) in Dec. 1776 was a major comeback after the loss of New York City; his army defeated the British in two battles and recaptured New Jersey.

The [Thirteen Colonies](#) began a rebellion against British rule in 1775 and proclaimed their independence in 1776 as the United States of America. In the [American Revolutionary War](#) (1775–83) the American captured the British invasion army at [Saratoga in 1777](#), secured the Northeast and encouraged the French to make a military alliance with the United States. France brought in Spain and the Netherlands, thus balancing the military and naval forces on each side as Britain had no allies.

General [George Washington](#) (1732–99) proved an excellent organizer and administrator, who worked successfully with Congress and the state governors, selecting and mentoring his senior officers, supporting and training his troops, and maintaining an idealistic Republican Army. His biggest challenge was logistics, since neither Congress nor the states had the funding to provide adequately for the equipment, [munitions](#), clothing, paychecks, or even the food supply of the soldiers.

As a battlefield tactician, Washington was often outmaneuvered by his British counterparts. As a strategist, however, he had a better idea of how to win the war than they did. The British sent four invasion armies. Washington's strategy forced the first army out of Boston in 1776, and was responsible for the surrender of the second and third armies at Saratoga (1777) and Yorktown (1781). He limited the British control to New York City and a few places while keeping Patriot control of the great majority of the population.

The Loyalists, whom the British counted upon too heavily, comprised about 20% of the population but never were well organized. As the war ended, Washington watched proudly as the final British army quietly sailed out of New York City in November 1783, taking the Loyalist leadership with them. Washington astonished the world when, instead of seizing power for himself, he retired quietly to his farm in Virginia.Political scientist Seymour Martin Lipset observes, "The United States was the first major colony successfully to revolt against colonial rule. In this sense, it was the first 'new nation'."

Trumbull's Declaration of Independence

On July 4, 1776, the Second Continental Congress, meeting in Philadelphia, declared the independence of "the United States of America" in theDeclaration of Independence. July 4 is celebrated as the nation's birthday. The new nation was founded on Enlightenment ideals of liberalism in what Thomas Jefferson called the unalienable rights to "life, liberty and the pursuit of happiness", and dedicated strongly to republicanprinciples. Republicanism emphasized the people are sovereign (not hereditary kings), demanded civic duty, feared corruption, and rejected any aristocracy.

Early years of the republic

History of the United States (1789–1849)

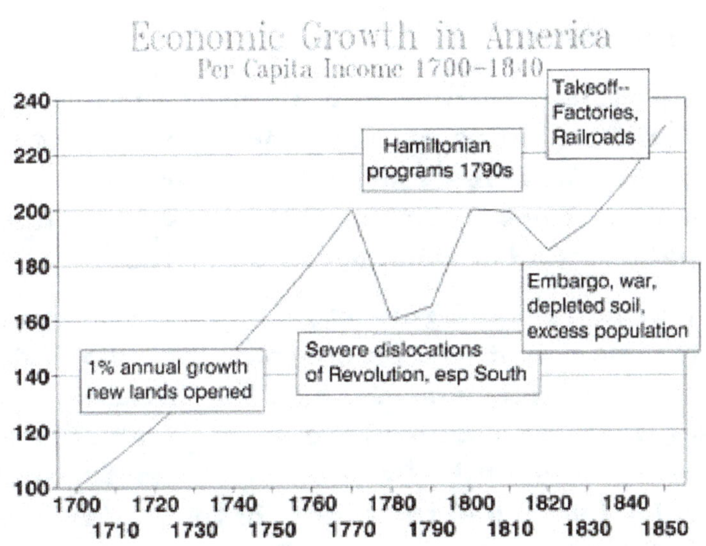

Economic growth in America per capita income; index with 1700 set as 100

Confederation and Constitution

In the 1780s the national government was able to settle the issue of the western territories, which were ceded by the states to Congress and became territories; with the migration of settlers to the Northwest, soon they became states. Nationalists worried that the new nation was too fragile to withstand an international war, or even internal revolts such as the [Shays' Rebellion](#) of 1786 in Massachusetts. Nationalists – most of them war veterans – organized in every state and convinced Congress to call the [Philadelphia Convention](#) in 1787. The delegates from every state wrote a new [Constitution](#) that created a much more powerful and efficient central government, one with a strong president, and powers of taxation. The new government reflected the prevailing republican ideals of guarantees of [individual liberty](#) and of constraining the power of government through a system of [separation of powers](#).

The Congress was given authority to ban the international [slave trade](#) after 20 years (which it did in 1807). A compromise gave the South Congressional apportionment out of proportion to its free population by allowing it to include three-fifths of the number of slaves in each state's total population. This provision increased the political power of southern representatives in Congress, especially as slavery was extended into the Deep South through removal of Native Americans and transportation of slaves by an extensive domestic trade.

To assuage the Anti-Federalists who feared a too-powerful national government, the nation adopted the [United States Bill of Rights](#) in 1791. Comprising the first ten amendments of the Constitution, it guaranteed individual liberties such as freedom of speech and religious practice, jury trials, and stated that citizens and states had reserved rights (which were not specified).

The New Chief Executive

[George Washington](#) – a renowned hero of the [American Revolutionary War](#), commander-in-chief of the [Continental Army](#), and president of the [Constitutional Convention](#) – became the first President of the United States under the new [Constitution](#) in 1789. The national capital moved from New York to Philadelphia and finally settled in Washington DC in 1800.

The major accomplishments of the [Washington Administration](#) were creating a strong national government that was recognized without question by all Americans. His government, following the vigorous leadership of Treasury Secretary [Alexander Hamilton](#), assumed the debts of the states (the debt holders received federal bonds), created the [Bank of the United States](#) to stabilize the financial system, and set up a uniform system of tariffs (taxes on imports) and other taxes to pay off the debt and provide a financial infrastructure. To support his programs Hamilton created a new political party – the first in the world based on voters – the [Federalist Party](#).

Thomas Jefferson and James Madison formed an opposition Republican Party (usually called the Democratic-Republican Party by political scientists). Hamilton and Washington presented the country in 1794 with the Jay Treaty that reestablished good relations with Britain. The Jeffersonians vehemently protested, and the voters aligned behind one party or the other, thus setting up the First Party System. Federalists promoted business, financial and commercial interests and wanted more trade with Britain. Republicans accused the Federalists of plans to establish a monarchy, turn the rich into a ruling class, and making the United States a pawn of the British. The treaty passed, but politics became intensely heated.

The Whiskey Rebellion in 1794, when western settlers protested against a federal tax on liquor, was the first serious test of the federal government. Washington called out the state militia and personally led an army, as the insurgents melted away and the power of the national government was firmly established. Washington refused to serve more than two terms – setting a precedent – and in his famous farewell address, he extolled the benefits of federal government and importance of ethics and morality while warning against foreign alliances and the formation of political parties.

John Adams, a Federalist, defeated Jefferson in the 1796 election. War loomed with France and the Federalists used the opportunity to try to silence the Republicans with the Alien and Sedition Acts, build up a large army with Hamilton at the head, and prepare for a French invasion. However, the Federalists became divided after Adams sent a successful peace mission to France that ended the Quasi-War of 1798.

Slavery
Slavery in the United States

During the first two decades after the Revolutionary War, there were dramatic changes in the status of slavery among the states and an increase in the number of freed blacks. Inspired by revolutionary ideals of the equality of men and influenced by their lesser economic reliance on slavery, northern states abolished slavery. Some had gradual emancipation schemes.

States of the Upper South made manumission easier, resulting in an increase in the proportion of free blacks in the Upper South (as a percentage of the total non-white population) from less than one percent in 1792 to more than 10 percent by 1810. By that date, a total of 13.5 percent of all blacks in the United States were free. After that date, with the demand for slaves on the rise because of the Deep South's expanding cotton cultivation, the number of manumissions declined sharply; and an internal U.S. slave trade became an important source of wealth for many planters and traders.

In 1809, president James Madison severed the U.S.A.'s involvement with the Atlantic slave trade.

19th century

Jeffersonian Republican Era

Jefferson saw himself as a man of the frontier and a scientist; he was keenly interested in expanding and exploring the West.

Territorial expansion; Louisiana Purchase in white.

Thomas Jefferson defeated Adams for the presidency in the 1800 election. Jefferson's major achievement as president was the Louisiana Purchase in 1803, which provided U.S. settlers with vast potential for expansion west of the Mississippi River.

Jefferson, a scientist himself, supported expeditions to explore and map the new domain, most notably the Lewis and Clark Expedition.Jefferson believed deeply in republicanism and argued it should be based on the independent yeoman farmer and planter; he distrusted cities, factories and banks. He also distrusted the federal government and judges, and tried to

weaken the judiciary. However he met his match in John Marshall, a Federalist from Virginia. Although the Constitution specified a Supreme Court, its functions were vague until Marshall, the Chief Justice (1801–35), defined them, especially the power to overturn acts of Congress or states that violated the Constitution, first enunciated in 1803 in *Marbury v. Madison*.

War of 1812

War of 1812

Americans were increasingly angry at the British violation of American ships' neutral rights in order to hurt France, the impressment (seizure) of 10,000 American sailors needed by the Royal Navy to fight Napoleon, and British support for hostile Indians attacking American settlers in the Midwest. They may also have desired to annex all or part of British North America. Despite strong opposition from the Northeast, especially from Federalists who did not want to disrupt trade with Britain, Congress declared war in June 18, 1812.The war was frustrating for both sides. Both sides tried to invade the other and were repulsed. The American high command remained incompetent until the last year. The American militia proved ineffective because the soldiers were reluctant to leave home and efforts to invade Canada repeatedly failed. The British blockade ruined American commerce, bankrupted the Treasury, and further angered New Englanders, who smuggled supplies to Britain. The Americans under General William Henry Harrison finally gained naval control of Lake Erie and defeated the Indians under Tecumseh in Canada, while Andrew Jackson ended the Indian threat in the Southeast. The Indian threat to expansion into the Midwest was permanently ended. The British invaded and occupied much of Maine.

The British raided and burned Washington, but were repelled at Baltimore in 1814 – where the "Star Spangled Banner" was written to celebrate the American success. In upstate New York a major British invasion of New York State was turned back. Finally in early 1815 Andrew Jackson decisively defeated a major British invasion at the Battle of New Orleans, making him the most famous war hero.

With Napoleon (apparently) gone, the causes of the war had evaporated and both sides agreed to a peace that left the prewar boundaries intact. Americans claimed victory in February 18, 1815 as news came almost simultaneously of Jackson's victory of New Orleans and the peace treaty that left the prewar boundaries in place. Americans swelled with pride at success in the "second war of independence"; the naysayers of the antiwar Federalist Party were put to shame and it never recovered. The Indians were the big losers; they never gained the independent nationhood Britain had promised and no longer posed a serious threat as settlers poured into the Midwest.

Era of Good Feelings

As strong opponents of the war, the Federalists held the Hartford Convention in 1814 that hinted at disunion. National euphoria after the victory at New Orleans ruined the prestige of the Federalists and they no longer played a significant role. President Madison and most Republicans realized they were foolish to let the Bank of the United States close down, for its absence greatly hindered the financing of the war. So, with the assistance of foreign bankers, they chartered the Second Bank of the United States in 1816.

The Republicans also imposed tariffs designed to protect the infant industries that had been created when Britain was blockading the U.S. With the collapse of the Federalists as a party, the adoption of many Federalist principles by the Republicans, and the systematic policy of President James Monroe in his two terms (1817–25) to downplay partisanship, the nation entered an Era of Good Feelings, with far less partisanship than before (or after), and closed out the First Party System.

The Monroe Doctrine, expressed in 1823, proclaimed the United States' opinion that European powers should no longer colonize or interfere in the Americas. This was a defining moment in the foreign policy of the United States. The Monroe Doctrine was adopted in response to American and British fears over Russian and French expansion into the Western Hemisphere.

In 1832, President Andrew Jackson, 7th President of the United States, ran for a second term under the slogan "Jackson and no bank" and didn't renew the charter of the Second Bank of the United States of America. Jackson was convinced that central banking was used by the elite to take advantage of the average American.

Indian removal

Settlers crossing the Plains of Nebraska.

In 1830, Congress passed the Indian Removal Act, which authorized the president to negotiate treaties that exchanged Native American tribal lands in the eastern states for lands west of the Mississippi River.Its goal was primarily to remove Native Americans, including theFive Civilized Tribes, from the American Southeast; they occupied land that settlers wanted. Jacksonian

Democrats demanded the forcible removal of native populations who refused to acknowledge state laws to reservations in the West; Whigs and religious leaders opposed the move as inhumane. Thousands of deaths resulted from the relocations, as seen in the Cherokee Trail of Tears. Many of the Seminole Indians in Florida refused to move west; they fought the Army for years in the Seminole Wars.

Second Party System

Second Party System

After the First Party System of Federalists and Republicans withered away in the 1820s, the stage was set for the emergence of a new party system based on very well organized local parties that appealed for the votes of (almost) all adult white men. The former Jeffersonian party split into factions. They split over the choice of a successor to President James Monroe, and the party faction that supported many of the old Jeffersonian principles, led by Andrew Jackson and Martin Van Buren, became the Democratic Party. As Norton explains the transformation in 1828:

> Jacksonians believed the people's will had finally prevailed. Through a lavishly financed coalition of state parties, political leaders, and newspaper editors, a popular movement had elected the president. The Democrats became the nation's first well-organized national party...and tight party organization became the hallmark of nineteenth-century American politics.

Opposing factions led by Henry Clay helped form the Whig Party. The Democratic Party had a small but decisive advantage over the Whigs until the 1850s, when the Whigs fell apart over the issue of slavery.

Behind the platforms issued by state and national parties stood a widely shared political outlook that characterized the Democrats:

The Democrats represented a wide range of views but shared a fundamental commitment to the Jeffersonian concept of an agrarian society. They viewed the central government as the enemy of individual liberty. The 1824 "corrupt bargain" had strengthened their suspicion of Washington politics....Jacksonians feared the concentration of economic and political power. They believed that government intervention in the economy benefited special-interest groups and created corporate monopolies that favored the rich. They sought to restore the independence of the individual--the artisan and the ordinary farmer--by ending federal support of banks and corporations and restricting the use of paper currency, which they distrusted. Their definition of the proper role of government tended to be negative, and Jackson's political power was largely expressed in negative acts. He exercised the veto more than all previous presidents combined. Jackson and his supporters also opposed reform as a movement. Reformers eager to turn their programs into legislation called for a more active government. But Democrats tended to oppose programs like educational reform mid the establishment of a public education system. They believed, for instance, that public schools restricted individual liberty by interfering with parental responsibility and undermined freedom of religion by replacing church schools. Nor did Jackson share reformers' humanitarian concerns. He had no sympathy for American Indians, initiating the removal of the Cherokees along the Trail of Tears.

Second Great Awakening

Second Great Awakening

The Second Great Awakening was a Protestant revival movement that affected the entire nation during the early 19th century and led to rapid church growth. The movement began around 1790, gained momentum by 1800, and, after 1820 membership rose rapidly among Baptist and Methodist congregations, whose preachers led the movement. It was past its peak by the 1840s.

It enrolled millions of new members in existing evangelical denominations and led to the formation of new denominations. Many converts believed that the Awakening heralded a new millennial age. The Second Great Awakening stimulated the establishment of many reform movements – including abolitionism and temperance designed to remove the evils of society before the anticipated Second Coming of Jesus Christ.

Abolitionism

After 1840 the growing abolitionist movement redefined itself as a crusade against the sin of slave ownership. It mobilized support (especially among religious women in the Northeast affected by the Second Great Awakening). William Lloyd Garrison published the most influential of the many anti-slavery newspapers, *The Liberator*, while Frederick Douglass, an ex-slave, began writing for that newspaper around 1840 and started his own abolitionist newspaper *North Star* in 1847. The great majority of anti-slavery activists, such as Abraham Lincoln, rejected Garrison's theology and held that slavery was an unfortunate social evil, not a sin.

Westward expansion and Manifest Destiny

American frontier

The American colonies and the new nation grew very rapidly in population and area, as pioneers pushed the frontier of settlement west.The process finally ended around 1890-1912 as the last major farmlands and ranch lands were settled. Native American tribes in some places resisted militarily, but they were overwhelmed by settlers and the army and after 1830 were relocated to reservations in the west. The highly influential "Frontier Thesis" argues that the frontier shaped the national character, with its boldness, violence, innovation,individualism, and democracy.

Recent historians have emphasized the multicultural nature of the frontier. Enormous popular attention in the media focuses on the "Wild West" of the second half of the 19th century. As defined by Hine and Faragher, "frontier history tells the story of the creation and defense of communities, the use of the land, the development of markets, and the formation of states". They explain, "It is a tale of conquest, but also one of survival, persistence, and the merging of peoples and cultures that gave birth and continuing life to America."Through wars and treaties, establishment of law and order, building farms, ranches, and towns, marking trails and digging mines, and pulling in great migrations of foreigners, the United States expanded from coast to coast fulfilling the dreams of Manifest Destiny. As the American frontier passed into history, the myths of the west in fiction and film took firm hold in the imagination of Americans and foreigners alike. America is exceptional in choosing its iconic self-image. "No other nation," says David Murdoch, "has taken a time and place from its past and produced a construct of the imagination equal to America's creation of the West."From the early 1830s to 1869, the Oregon Trail and its many offshoots were used by over 300,000 settlers. '49ers (in the California Gold Rush), ranchers, farmers, and entrepreneurs and their families headed to California, Oregon, and other points in the far west. Wagon-trains took five or six months on foot; after 1869, the trip took 6 days by rail.

American occupation of Mexico Cityduring the Mexican–American War.

Manifest Destiny was the belief that American settlers were destined to expand across the continent. This concept was born out of "A sense of mission to redeem the Old World by high example... generated by the potentialities of a new earth for building a new heaven."Manifest Destiny was rejected by modernizers, especially the Whigs like Henry Clay and Abraham Lincoln who wanted to build cities and factories – not more farms. However Democrats strongly favored expansion, and they won the key election of 1844. After a bitter debate in Congress the Republic of Texas was annexed in 1845, which Mexico had warned meant war. War broke out in 1846, with the homefront polarized as Whigs opposed and Democrats supported the war. The U.S. army, using regulars and large numbers of volunteers, won the Mexican-American War (1846–48). The 1848 Treaty of Guadalupe Hidalgo made peace; Mexico recognized the annexation of Texas and ceded its claims in the Southwest (especially California and New Mexico). The Hispanic residents were given full citizenship and the Mexican Indians became American Indians. Simultaneously gold was discovered, pulling over 100,000 men to northern California in a matter of months in the California Gold Rush. Not only did the then president James K. Polk expand America's border to theRepublic of Texas and a fraction of Mexico but he also annexed the north western frontier known as the Oregon Country, which was renamed the Oregon Territory.

Divisions between North and South

Origins of the American Civil War and *American Civil War*

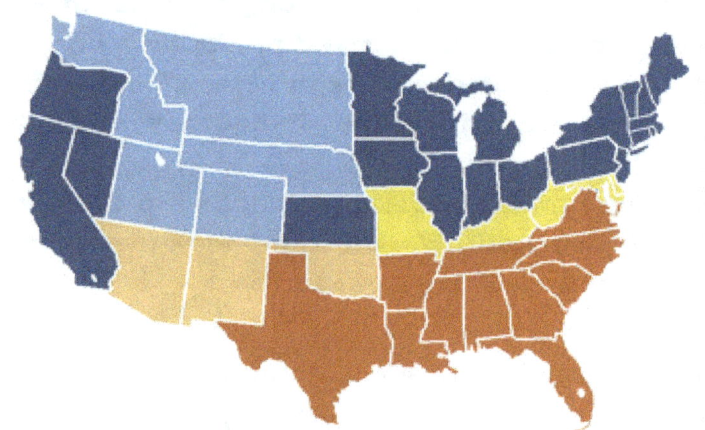

Union states: navy blue (free) and yellow (slave)

Confederacy states: brown (slave)

U.S. territories: lighter shades of blue and brown

The central issue after 1848 was the expansion of slavery, pitting the anti-slavery elements that were a majority in the North, against the pro-slavery elements that overwhelmingly dominated the white South. A small number of very active Northerners were abolitionists who declared that ownership of slaves was a sin (in terms of Protestant theology) and demanded its immediate abolition. Much larger numbers were against the expansion of slavery, seeking to put it on the path to extinction so that America would be committed to free land (as in low-cost farms owned and cultivated by a family), free labor (no slaves), and free speech (as opposed to censorship rampant in the South). Southern whites insisted that slavery was of economic, social, and cultural benefit to all whites (and even to the slaves themselves), and denounced all anti-slavery spokesmen as "abolitionists."

Religious activists split on slavery, with the Methodists and Baptists dividing into northern and southern denominations. In the North, the Methodists, Congregationalists, and Quakers included many abolitionists, especially among women activists. (The Catholic, Episcopal and Lutheran denominations largely ignored the slavery issue.)

The issue of slavery in the new territories was seemingly settled by the Compromise of 1850, brokered by Whig Henry Clayand Democrat Stephen Douglas; the Compromise included the admission of California as a free state. The point of contention was the Fugitive Slave Act, which increased federal enforcement and required even free states to cooperate in turning over fugitive slaves to their owners. Abolitionists pounced on the Act to attack slavery, as in the best-selling anti-slavery novel *Uncle Tom's Cabin* by Harriet Beecher Stowe.

The Compromise of 1820 was repealed in 1854 with the Kansas-Nebraska Act, promoted by Senator Douglas in the name of "popular sovereignty" and democracy. It permitted voters to decide on slavery in each territory, and allowed Douglas to say he was neutral on the slavery issue. Anti-slavery forces rose in anger and alarm, forming the new Republican Party. Pro- and anti- contingents rushed to Kansas to vote slavery up or down, resulting in a miniature civil war called Bleeding Kansas. By the late 1850s, the young Republican Party dominated nearly all northern states and thus the electoralcollege. It insisted that slavery would never be allowed to expand (and thus would slowly die out).

The Southern slavery-based societies had become wealthy based on their cotton and other agricultural commodity production, and some particularly profited from the internal slave trade. Northern cities such as Boston and New York, and regional industries, were tied economically to slavery by banking, shipping, and manufacturing, including textile mills. By 1860, there were four million slaves in the South, nearly eight times as many as there were nationwide in 1790. The plantations were highly profitable, because of the heavy European demand for raw cotton. Most of the profits were invested in new lands and in purchasing more slaves (largely drawn from the declining tobacco regions).

For 50 of the nation's first 72 years, a slaveholder served as President of the United States and, during that period, only slaveholding presidents were re-elected to second terms. In addition, southern states benefited by their increased apportionment in Congress due to the partial counting of slaves in their populations.

Slave rebellions were planned or actually took place – including by Gabriel Prosser (1800), Denmark Vesey (1822), Nat Turner (1831), and John Brown (1859) – but they only involved dozens of people and all failed. They caused fear in the white South, which imposed tighter slave oversight and reduced the rights of free blacks. The Fugitive Slave Act of 1850 required the states to cooperate with slave owners when attempting to recover escaped slaves, which outraged Northerners. Formerly, an escaped slave, having reached a non-slave state, was presumed to have attained sanctuary and freedom. The Supreme Court's 1857 decision in *Dred Scott v. Sandford* ruled that the Missouri Compromise was unconstitutional; angry Republicans said this decision threatened to make slavery a national institution.

After Abraham Lincoln won the 1860 election, seven Southern states seceded from the union and set up a new nation, the Confederate States of America (C.S.A.), on February 8, 1861. It attacked Fort Sumter, a U.S. Army fort in South Carolina, thus igniting the war. When Lincoln called for troops to suppress the Confederacy in April 1861, four more states seceded and joined the Confederacy. A few of the (northernmost) "slave states" did not secede and became known as the border states; these were Delaware, Maryland, Kentucky, and Missouri.

During the war, the northwestern portion of Virginia seceded from the C.S.A. and became the new Union state of West Virginia. West Virginia is usually grouped with the border states.

Civil War
American Civil War

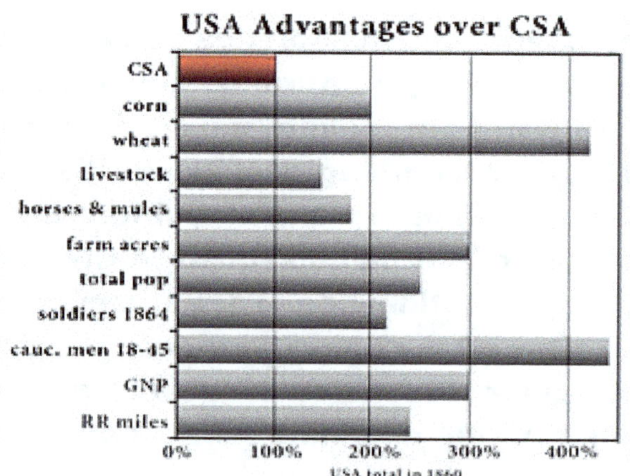

The Union had large advantages in men and resources at the start of the war; the ratio grew steadily in favor of the Union

The Civil War began on April 12, 1861, when Confederate forces attacked a U.S. military installation at Fort Sumter in South Carolina. In response to the attack, on April 15, Lincoln called on the states to send detachments totaling 75,000 troops to recapture forts, protect the capital, and "preserve the Union", which in his view still existed intact despite the actions of the seceding states. The two armies had their first major clash at the First Battle of Bull Run, ending in a Union defeat, but, more importantly, proved to both the Union and Confederacy that the war would be much longer and bloodier than originally anticipated.

Lincoln with Allan Pinkerton and Major GeneralJohn Alexander McClernandat the Battle of Antietam.

The war soon divided into two theaters: Eastern and Western. In the western theater, the Union was quite successful, with major battles, such as Perryville and Shiloh, producing strategic Union victories and destroying major Confederate operations.

Irish anger at the draft led to the New York Draft Riots of 1863, one of the worst incidents of civil unrest in American history

Warfare in the Eastern theater started poorly for the Union as the Confederates won at Manassas Junction (Bull Run), just outside Washington. Major General George B. McClellan was put in charge of the

Union armies. After reorganizing the new Army of the Potomac, McClellan failed to capture the Confederate capital of Richmond, Virginia in his Peninsula Campaign and retreated after attacks from newly appointed Confederate General Robert E. Lee.

Feeling confident in his army after defeating the Union at Second Bull Run, Lee embarked on aninvasion of the north that was stopped by McClellan at the bloody Battle of Antietam. Despite this, McClellan was relieved from command for refusing to pursue Lee's crippled army. The next commander, General Ambrose Burnside, suffered a humiliating defeat by Lee's smaller army at the Battle of Fredericksburg late in 1862, causing yet another change in commanders. Lee won again at the Battle of Chancellorsville in May 1863, while losing his top aide, Stonewall Jackson. But Lee pushed too hard and ignored the Union threat in the west. Lee invaded Pennsylvania in search of supplies and to cause war-weariness in the North. In perhaps the turning point of the war, Lee's army was badly beaten at the Battle of Gettysburg, July 1–3, 1863, and barely made it back to Virginia.

Battle of Franklin, November 30, 1864

Simultaneously on July 4, 1863, Union forces under the command of General Ulysses S. Grant gained control of the Mississippi River at the Battle of Vicksburg, thereby splitting the Confederacy. Lincoln made General Grant commander of all Union armies.

The last two years of the war were bloody for both sides, with Grant launching a war of attrition against General Lee's Army of Northern Virginia. This war of attrition was divided into three main campaigns. The first of these, the Overland Campaign forced Lee to retreat into the city of Petersburg where Grant launched his second major offensive, the Richmond-Petersburg Campaign in which he besieged Petersburg. After a near ten-month siege, Petersburg surrendered. However, the defense of Fort Gregg allowed Lee to move his army out of Petersburg. Grant pursued and launched the final, Appomattox Campaign which resulted in Lee surrendering his Army of Northern Virginia on April 9, 1865, at [Appomattox Court House](). Other Confederate armies followed suit and the war ended with no postwar insurgency.

Based on [1860 census]() figures, about 8% of all white males aged 13 to 43 died in the war, including 6% from the North and 18% from the South, establishing the American Civil War as the deadliest war in American history. Its legacy includes ending slavery in the United States, restoring the Union, and strengthening the role of the federal government.

Reconstruction

[History of the United States (1865–1918)]()

[Reconstruction era of the United States]()

[Freedmen]() voting in New Orleans, 1867

Reconstruction lasted from Lincoln's [Emancipation Proclamation]() of January 1, 1863 to the [Compromise of 1877]().

The major issues faced by Lincoln were the status of the ex-slaves (called "Freedmen"), the loyalty and civil rights of ex-rebels, the status of the 11 ex-Confederate states, the powers of the federal government needed to prevent a future civil war, and the question of whether Congress or the President would make the major decisions.

The severe threats of starvation and displacement of the unemployed Freedmen were met by the first major federal relief agency, the [Freedmen's Bureau](), operated by the Army.

Three "[Reconstruction Amendments]()" were passed to expand civil rights for black Americans: the [Thirteenth Amendment]() outlawed slavery; the [Fourteenth Amendment]() guaranteed equal rights for all and citizenship for blacks; the [Fifteenth Amendment]() prevented race from being used to disfranchise men.

Ex-Confederates remained in control of most Southern states for over two years, but that changed when the [Radical Republicans]() gained control of Congress in the 1866 elections. President [Andrew Johnson](), who sought easy terms for reunions with ex-rebels, was virtually powerless; he escaped by one vote removal through impeachment. Congress enfranchised black men and temporarily stripped many ex-Confederate leaders of the right to hold office. New Republican governments came to power based on a coalition of Freedmen made up of Carpetbaggers (new arrivals from the North), and Scalawags (native white Southerners). They were backed by the US Army. Opponents said they were corrupt and violated the rights of whites. State by state they lost power to a conservative-Democratic coalition, which gained control of the entire South by 1877. In response to Radical Reconstruction, the Ku Klux Klan (KKK) emerged in 1867 as a white-supremacist organization opposed to black civil rights and Republican rule. President Ulysses Grant's vigorous enforcement of the Ku Klux Klan Act of 1870 shut down the Klan, and it disbanded. Paramilitary groups, such as the White League and Red Shirts emerged about 1874 that worked openly to use intimidation and violence to suppress black voting to regain white political power in states across the South during the 1870s. Rable described them as the military arm of the Democratic Party. Reconstruction ended after the disputed 1876 election between Republican candidate Rutherford B. Hayes and Democratic candidate Samuel J. Tilden. With a compromise Hayes won the White House, the federal government withdrew its troops from the South, and Southern Democrats re-entered the national political scene. From 1890 to 1908, southern states effectively disfranchised most black voters and many poor whites by making voter registration more difficult through poll taxes, literacy tests, and other arbitrary devices. They passed segregation laws and imposed second-class status on blacks in a system known as Jim Crow that lasted until the successes of the Civil Rights movement in 1964-65.

Deeply religious Southerners saw the hand of God in history, which demonstrated His wrath at their sinfulness, or His rewards for their suffering. Historian Wilson Falling has examined the sermons of white and black Baptist preachers after the War. Southern white preachers said:

God had chastised them and given them a special mission – to maintain orthodoxy, strict Biblicism, personal piety, and traditional race relations. Slavery, they insisted, had not been sinful. Rather, emancipation was a historical tragedy and the end of Reconstruction was a clear sign of God's favor.

In sharp contrast, Black preachers interpreted the Civil War as:

God's gift of freedom. They appreciated opportunities to exercise their independence, to worship in their own way, to affirm their worth and dignity, and to proclaim the fatherhood of God and the brotherhood of man. Most of all, they could form their own churches, associations, and conventions. These institutions offered self-help and racial uplift, and provided places where the gospel of liberation could be proclaimed. As a result, black preachers continued to insist that God would protect and help him; God would be their rock in a stormy land.

The West and the Gilded Age

Completion of the Transcontinental Railroad (1869) at First Transcontinental Railroad, by Andrew J. Russell.

Gilded Age

The latter half of the nineteenth century was marked by the rapid development and settlement of the far West, first by wagon trains and riverboats and then aided by the completion of the transcontinental railroad. Large numbers of European immigrants (especially from Germany and Scandinavia) took up low-cost or free farms in the Prairie States. Mining for silver and copper opened up the Mountain West. The United States Army fought frequent small-scale wars with Native Americans as settlers encroached on their traditional lands. Gradually the US purchased the Native American tribal lands and extinguished their claims, forcing most tribes onto subsidized reservations. According to the U.S. Bureau of the Census (1894), from 1789 to 1894:

> The Indian wars under the government of the United States have been more than 40 in number. They have cost the lives of about 19,000 white men, women and children, including those killed in individual combats, and the lives of about 30,000 Indians. The actual number of killed and wounded Indians must be very much higher than the given... Fifty percent additional would be a safe estimate...

The "Gilded Age" was a term that Mark Twain used to describe the period of the late 19th century when there had been a dramatic expansion of American wealth and prosperity. Reform of the Age included the Civil Service Act, which mandated a competitive examination for applicants for government jobs. Other important legislation included the Interstate Commerce Act, which ended railroads' discrimination against small shippers, and the Sherman Antitrust Act, which outlawed monopolies in business. Twain believed that this age was corrupted by such elements as land speculators, scandalous politics, and unethical business practices. Since the days of Charles A. Beard and Matthew Josephson, some historians have argued that the United States was effectively plutocratic for at least part of the Gilded Age and Progressive Era. As financiers and industrialists such as J.P. Morgan and John D. Rockefeller began to amass vast fortunes, many US observers were concerned that the nation was losing its pioneering egalitarian spirit.

By 1890 American industrial production and per capita income exceeded those of all other world nations. In response to heavy debts and decreasing farm prices, wheat and cotton farmers joined the Populist Party. An unprecedented wave of immigration from Europe served to both provide the labor for American industry and create diverse communities in previously undeveloped areas. From 1880 to 1914, peak years of immigration, more than 22 million people migrated to the United States. Most were unskilled workers who quickly found jobs in mines, mills, factories. Many immigrants were craftsmen (especially from Britain and Germany) bringing human skills, and others were farmers (especially from Germany and Scandinavia) who purchased inexpensive land on the Prairies from railroads who sent agents to Europe. Poverty, growing inequality and dangerous working conditions, along withsocialist and anarchist ideas diffusing from European immigrants, led to the rise of the labor movement, which often included violent strikes.Skilled workers banded together to control their crafts and raise wages by forming labor unions in industrial areas of the Northeast. Before the 1930s few factory workers joined theunions in the labor movement. Samuel Gompers led the American Federation of Labor 1886-1924, coordinating multiple unions. Industrial growth was very rapid, led by John D. Rockefeller in oil and Andrew Carnegie in steel; both became leaders of philanthropy, giving away their fortunes to create the modern system of hospitals, universities, libraries, and foundations.

Mulberry Street, along which Manhattan's Little Italy is centered. Lower East Side, circa 1900. Almost 97% of residents of the 10 largest American cities of 1900 were non-Hispanic whites.

A severe nationwide depression broke out in 1893; it was called the Panic of 1893 and impacted farmers, workers, and businessmen who saw prices, wages, and profits fall. Many railroads went bankrupt. The resultant political reaction fell on the Democratic Party, whose leader President Grover Cleveland shouldered much of the blame. Labor unrest involved numerous strikes, most notably the violent Pullman Strike of 1894, which was shut down by federal troops under Cleveland's orders. The Populist Party gained strength among cotton and wheat farmers, as well as coal miners, but was overtaken by the even more popular Free Silver movement, which demanded using silver to enlarge the money supply, leading to inflation that the silverites promised would end the depression. The financial, railroad, and business communities fought back hard, arguing that only the gold standard would save the economy. In the most intense election in the nation's history, conservative Republican William McKinley defeated silverite William Jennings Bryan, who ran on the Democratic, Populist, and Silver Republican tickets. Bryan swept the South and West, but McKinley ran up landslides among the middle class, industrial workers, cities, and among upscale farmers in the Midwest.

Prosperity returned under McKinley, the gold standard was enacted, and the tariff was raised. By 1900 the US had the strongest economy on the globe. Apart from two short recessions (in 1907 and 1920) the overall economy remained prosperous and growing until 1929. Republicans, citing McKinley's policies, took the credit.

20th century

Progressive Era

Dissatisfaction on the part of the growing middle class with the corruption and inefficiency of politics as usual, and the failure to deal with increasingly important urban and industrial problems, led to the dynamic Progressive Movement starting in the 1890s. In every major city and state, and at the national level as well, and in education, medicine, and industry, the progressives called for the modernization and reform of decrepit institutions, the elimination of corruption in politics, and the introduction of efficiency as a criterion for change. Leading politicians from both parties, most notably Theodore Roosevelt, Charles Evans Hughes, and Robert LaFollette on the Republican side, and William Jennings Bryan and Woodrow Wilson on the Democratic side, took up the cause of progressive reform. Women became especially involved in demands for woman suffrage, prohibition, and better schools; their most prominent leader was Jane Addams of Chicago. "Muckraking" journalists such as Upton Sinclair, Lincoln Steffens and Jacob Riis exposed corruption in business and government along with rampant inner city poverty. Progressives implemented anti-trust laws and regulated such industries of meat-packing, drugs, and railroads. Four new constitutional amendments – the Sixteenth through Nineteenth – resulted from progressive activism, bringing the federal income tax, direct election of Senators, prohibition, and woman suffrage.The Progressive Movement lasted through the 1920s; the most active period was 1900–18.

Imperialism

The United States emerged as a world economic and military power after 1890. The main episode was the Spanish–American War, which began when Spain refused American demands to reform its oppressive policies in Cuba. The "splendid little war", as one official called it, involved a series of quick American victories on land and at sea. At the Treaty of Paris peace conference the United States acquired the Philippines, Puerto Rico, and Guam.Cuba became an independent country, under close American tutelage. Although the war itself was widely popular, the peace terms proved controversial. William Jennings Bryan led his Democratic Party in opposition to control of the Philippines, which he denounced as imperialism unbecoming to American democracy. President William McKinley defended the acquisition and was riding high as the nation had returned to prosperity and felt triumphant in the war. McKinley easily defeated Bryan in a rematch in the 1900 presidential election.

After defeating an insurrection by Filipino nationalists, the United States engaged in a large-scale program to modernize the economy of the Philippines and dramatically upgrade the public health facilities. By 1908, however, Americans lost interest in an empire and turned their international attention to the Caribbean, especially the building of the Panama Canal. In 1912 when Arizona became the final mainland state, the American Frontier came to an end. The canal opened in 1914 and increased trade with Japan and the rest of the Far East. A key innovation was the Open Door Policy, whereby the imperial powers were given equal access to Chinese business, with not one of them allowed to take control of China.

World War I

American entry into World War I and *United States home front during World War I*

American Cemetery at Romagne-sous-Montfaucon

As World War I raged in Europe from 1914, President Woodrow Wilson took full control of foreign policy, declaring neutrality but warning Germany that resumption of unrestricted submarine warfare against American ships supplying goods to Allied nations would mean war. Germany decided to take the risk and try to win by cutting off supplies to Britain; the U.S. declared war in April 1917. American money, food, and munitions arrived quickly, but troops had to be drafted and trained; by summer 1918 American soldiers under General John J. Pershingarrived at the rate of 10,000 a day, while Germany was unable to replace its losses.

The result was Allied victory in November 1918. President Wilson demanded Germany depose the Kaiser and accept his terms, the Fourteen Points. Wilson dominated the 1919 Paris Peace Conference but Germany was treated harshly by the Allies in the Treaty of Versailles (1919) as Wilson put all his hopes in the new League of Nations. Wilson refused to compromise with Senate Republicans over the issue of Congressional power to declare war, and the Senate rejected the Treaty and the League.

Women's suffrage

Women's suffrage in the United States

Alice Paul wrote the Equal Rights Amendment, whose passage became an unachieved goal of the feminist movement in the 1970s

The women's suffrage movement began with the June 1848 National Convention of the Liberty Party. Presidential candidate Gerrit Smith argued for and established women's suffrage as a party plank. One month later, his cousin Elizabeth Cady Stanton joined with Lucretia Mott and other women to organize the Seneca Falls Convention, featuring the Declaration of Sentiments demanding equal rights for women, and the right to vote.Many of these activists became politically aware during the abolitionist movement. The women's rights campaign during "first-wave feminism" was led by Stanton, Lucy Stone and Susan B. Anthony, among many others. Stone and Paulina Wright Davis organized the prominent and influential National Women's Rights Convention in 1850. The movement reorganized after the Civil War, gaining experienced campaigners, many of whom had worked for prohibition in the Women's Christian Temperance Union. By the end of the 19th century a few western states had granted women full voting rights,though women had made significant legal victories, gaining rights in areas such as property and child custody.

Around 1912 the feminist movement, which had grown sluggish, began to reawaken, putting an emphasis on its demands for equality and arguing that the corruption of American politics demanded purification by women because men could not do that job. Protests became increasingly common as suffragette Alice Paul led parades through the capital and major cities. Paul split from the large National American Woman Suffrage Association(NAWSA), which favored a more moderate approach and supported the Democratic Party and Woodrow Wilson, led by Carrie Chapman Catt, and formed the more militant National Woman's Party. Suffragists were arrested during their "Silent Sentinels" pickets at the White House, the first time such a tactic was used, and were taken as political prisoners.

The old anti-suffragist argument that only men could fight a war, and therefore only men deserve the right to vote, was refuted by the enthusiastic participation of tens of thousands of American women on the home front in World War I. Across the world, grateful nations gave women the right to vote. Furthermore, most of the Western states had already given the women the right to vote in state and national elections, and the representatives from those states, including the first woman Jeannette Rankin of Montana, demonstrated that woman suffrage was a success. The main resistance came from the south, where white leaders were worried about the threat of black women voting. Congress passed the Nineteenth Amendment in 1919, and women could vote in 1920.

NAWSA became the League of Women Voters, and the National Woman's Party began lobbying for full equality and the Equal Rights Amendment, which would pass Congress during the second wave of the women's movement in 1972. Politicians responded to the new electorate by emphasizing issues of special interest to women, especially prohibition, child health, and world peace. The main surge of women voting came in 1928, when the big-city machines realized they needed the support of women to elect Al Smith, a Catholic from New York City. Meanwhile Protestants mobilized women to support Prohibition and vote for Republican Herbert Hoover.

Roaring Twenties and the Great Depression
History of the United States (1918–45)

Great Depression and *New Deal*

Prohibition agents destroying barrels of alcohol in Chicago, 1921

In the 1920s the U.S. grew steadily in stature as an economic and military world power. The United States Senate did not ratify the Treaty of Versailles imposed by its Allies on the defeated Central Powers; instead, the United States chose to pursue unilateralism. The aftershock of Russia's October Revolution resulted in real fears of Communism in the United States, leading to a Red Scare and the deportation of aliens considered subversive.

While public health facilities grew rapidly in the Progressive Era, and hospitals and medical schools were modernized, the nation in 1918 lost 675,000 lives to the Spanish flu pandemic.

In 1920, the manufacture, sale, import and export of alcohol were prohibited by the Eighteenth Amendment, Prohibition. The result was that in cities illegal alcohol became a big business, largely controlled by racketeers. The second Ku Klux Klan grew rapidly in 1922-25, then collapsed. Immigration laws were passed to strictly limit the number of new entries. The 1920s were called the Roaring Twenties due to the great economic prosperity during this period. Jazz became popular among the younger generation, and thus the decade was also called the Jazz Age.

The Great Depression (1929–39) and the New Deal (1933–36) were decisive moments in American political, economic, and social history that reshaped the nation.

During the 1920s, the nation enjoyed widespread prosperity, albeit with a weakness in agriculture. A financial bubble was fueled by an inflated stock market, which later led to the Stock Market Crash on October 29, 1929. This, along with many other economic factors, triggered a worldwidedepression known as the Great Depression. During this time, the United States experienced deflation as prices fell, unemployment soared from 3% in 1929 to 25% in 1933, farm prices fell by half, and manufacturing output plunged by one-third.

In 1932, Democratic presidential nominee Franklin D. Roosevelt promised "a New Deal for the American people", coining the enduring label for his domestic policies. The desperate economic situation, along with the substantial Democratic victories in the 1932 elections, gave Roosevelt unusual influence over Congress in the "First Hundred Days" of his administration. He used his leverage to win rapid passage of a series of measures to create welfare programs and regulate the banking system, stock market, industry, and agriculture, along with many other government efforts to end the Great Depression and reform the American economy. The New Deal regulated much of the economy, especially the financial sector. It provided relief to the unemployed through numerous programs, such as the Works Progress Administration (WPA) and (for young men) the Civilian Conservation Corps. Large scale spending projects designed to provide high paying jobs and rebuild the infrastructure were under the purview of the Public Works Administration. Roosevelt turned left in 1935–36, building up labor unions through the Wagner Act. Unions became a powerful element of the mergingNew Deal Coalition, which won reelection for Roosevelt in 1936, 1940, and 1944 by mobilizing union members, blue collar workers, relief recipients, big city machines, ethnic, and religious groups (especially Catholics and Jews) and the white South, along with blacks in the North (where they could vote). Some of the programs were dropped in the 1940s when the conservatives regained power in Congress through the Conservative Coalition. Of special importance is the Social Security program, begun in 1935.

World War II

The Japanese crippled American naval power with the attack on Pearl Harbor, knocking out all the battleships

World War II, *Military history of the United States during World War II* and *United States home front during World War II*

In the Depression years, the United States remained focused on domestic concerns while democracy declined across the world and many countries fell under the control of dictators. Imperial Japan asserted dominance in East Asia and in the Pacific. Nazi Germany and Fascist Italymilitarized too and threatened conquests, while Britain and France attempted appeasement to avert another war in Europe. US legislation in theNeutrality Acts sought to avoid foreign conflicts; however, policy clashed with increasing anti-Nazi feelings following the German invasion of Poland in September 1939 that started World War II. Roosevelt positioned the US as the "Arsenal of Democracy", pledging full-scale financial and munitions support for the Allies – but no military personnel.[136] Japan tried to neutralize America's power in the Pacific by attacking Pearl Harbor on December 7, 1941, which catalyzed American support to enter the war and seek revenge.[137]

The main contributions of the US to the Allied war effort comprised money, industrial output, food, petroleum, technological innovation, and (especially 1944–45), military personnel. Much of the focus in Washington was maximizing the economic output of the nation. The overall result was a dramatic increase in GDP, the export of vast quantities of supplies to the Allies and to American forces overseas, the end of unemployment, and a rise in civilian consumption even as 40% of the GDP went to the war effort. This was achieved by tens of millions of workers moving from low-productivity occupations to high efficiency jobs, improvements in productivity through better technology and management, and the move into the active labor force of students, retired people, housewives, and the unemployed, and an increase in hours worked.

Into the Jaws of Death: The Normandy landings began the Allied march toward Germany from the west.

American corpses sprawled on the beach of Tarawa, November 1943.

It was exhausting; leisure activities declined sharply. People tolerated the extra work because of patriotism, the pay, and the confidence that it was only "for the duration", and life would return to normal as soon as the war was won. Most durable goods became unavailable, and meat, clothing, and gasoline were tightly rationed. In industrial areas housing was in short supply as people doubled up and lived in cramped quarters. Prices and wages were controlled, and Americans saved a high portion of their incomes, which led to renewed growth after the war instead of a return to depression.

The Allies – the US, Britain, and the Soviet Union, as well as China, Canada and other countries – fought the Axis powers of Germany, Italy, and Japan. The Allies saw Germany as the main threat and gave highest priority to Europe. The US dominated the war against Japan and stopped Japanese expansion in the Pacific in 1942. After losing Pearl Harbor and in the Philippines to the Japanese, and drawing the Battle of the Coral Sea (May 1942), the American Navy inflicted a decisive blow at Midway (June 1942). American ground forces assisted in the North African Campaign that eventually concluded with the collapse of Mussolini's fascist government in

1943, as Italy switched to the Allied side. A more significant European front was opened on D-Day, June 6, 1944, in which American and Allied forces invaded Nazi-occupied France from Britain.

Bronze statue ofEisenhower at Capitol rotunda.

On the home front, mobilization of the US economy was managed by Roosevelt's War Production Board. The wartime production boom led to full employment, wiping out this vestige of the Great Depression. Indeed, labor shortages encouraged industry to look for new sources of workers, finding new roles for women and blacks.However, the fervor also inspired anti-Japanese sentiment, which was handled by removing everyone of Japanese descent from the West Coast war zone. Research and development took flight as well, best seen in the Manhattan Project, a secret effort to harness nuclear fission to produce highly destructive atomic bombs.The Allied pushed the Germans out of France but faced an unexpected counterattack at the Battle of the Bulge in December. The final German effort failed, and, as Allied armies in East and West were converging on Berlin, the Nazis hurriedly tried to kill the last remaining Jews. The western front stopped short, leaving Berlin to the Soviets as the Nazi regime formally capitulated in May 1945, ending the war in Europe.Over in the Pacific, the US implemented an island hopping strategy toward Tokyo, establishing airfields for bombing runs against mainland Japan from the Mariana Islands and achieving hard-fought victories at Iwo Jima and Okinawa in 1945. Bloodied at Okinawa, the U.S. prepared to invade Japan's home islands when B-29sdropped atomic

bombs on the Japanese cities of **Hiroshima** and **Nagasaki**, forcing the empire's surrender in a matter of days and thus ending World War II. The US occupied Japan (and part of Germany), sending **Douglas MacArthur** to restructure the Japanese economy and political system along American lines.

Though the nation lost more than 400,000 military personnel, the mainland prospered untouched by the devastation of war that inflicted a heavy toll on Europe and Asia.

Participation in postwar foreign affairs marked the end of predominant American isolationism. The awesome threat of nuclear weapons inspired both**optimism** and **fear**. Nuclear weapons were never used after 1945, as both sides drew back from the brink and a "long peace" characterized the **Cold War** years, starting with the**Truman Doctrine** in May 22, 1947. There were, however, regional wars in **Korea** and **Vietnam**.

The Cold War, counterculture, and civil rights

History of the United States (1945–64), *History of the United States (1964–80)* and *United States in the 1950s*

President Kennedy's **Civil Rights Address**, June 11, 1963.

Following World War II, the United States emerged as one of the two dominant superpowers, the **USSR** being the other. The **U.S. Senate** on a bipartisan vote approved U.S. participation in the United Nations (UN), which marked a turn away from the traditional **isolationism** of the U.S. and toward increased international involvement.

The primary American goal of 1945–48 was to rescue Europe from the devastation of World War II and to contain the expansion of Communism, represented by the Soviet Union. The Truman Doctrine of 1947 provided military and economic aid to Greece and Turkey to counteract the threat of Communist expansion in the Balkans. In 1948, the United States replaced piecemeal financial aid programs with a comprehensive Marshall Plan, which pumped money into the economy of Western Europe, and removed trade barriers, while modernizing the managerial practices of businesses and governments.The Plan's $13 billion budget was in the context of a US GDP of $258 billion in 1948 and was in addition to the $12 billion in American aid given to Europe between the end of the war and the start of the Marshall Plan. Soviet head of state Joseph Stalin prevented his satellite states from participating, and from that point on, Eastern Europe, with inefficient centralized economies, fell further and further behind Western Europe in terms of economic development and prosperity. In 1949, the United States, rejecting the long-standing policy of no military alliances in peacetime, formed the North Atlantic Treaty Organization (NATO) alliance, which continues into the 21st century. In response the Soviets formed the Warsaw Pact of communist states.

In August 1949 the Soviets tested their first nuclear weapon, thereby escalating the risk of warfare. Indeed, the threat of mutually assured destruction prevented both powers from going too far, and resulted in proxy wars, especially in Korea and Vietnam, in which the two sides did not directly confront each other. Within the United States, the Cold War prompted concerns about Communist influence. The unexpected leapfrogging of American technology by the Soviets in 1957 with Sputnik, the first Earth satellite, began the Space Race, won by the Americans as Apollo 11 landed astronauts on the moon in 1969. The angst about the weaknesses of American education led to large-scale federal support for science education and research.

In the decades after World War II, the United States became a global influence in economic, political, military, cultural, and technological affairs. Beginning in the 1950s, middle-class culture became obsessed with consumer goods. White Americans made up nearly 90% of the population in 1950.In 1960, the charismatic politician John F. Kennedy was elected as the first and – thus far – only Roman Catholic President of the United States. The Kennedy family brought a new life and vigor to the atmosphere of the White House. His time in office was marked by such notable events as the acceleration of the United States' role in the Space Race, escalation of the American role in the Vietnam War, the Cuban missile crisis, the Bay of Pigs Invasion, the jailing of Martin Luther King, Jr. during the Birmingham campaign, and the appointment of his brother Robert F. Kennedy to his Cabinet as Attorney General. Kennedy was assassinated in Dallas, Texas, on November 22, 1963, leaving the nation in profound shock.

Climax of liberalism

The climax of liberalism came in the mid-1960s with the success of President Lyndon B. Johnson (1963–69) in securing congressional passage of his Great Society programs.They included civil rights, the end of segregation, Medicare, extension of welfare, federal aid to education at all levels, subsidies for the arts and humanities, environmental activism, and a series of programs designed to wipe out poverty. As recent historians have explained:

> Gradually, liberal intellectuals crafted a new vision for achieving economic and social justice. The liberalism of the early 1960s contained no hint of radicalism, little disposition to revive new deal era crusades against concentrated economic power, and no intention to fast and class passions or redistribute wealth or restructure existing institutions. Internationally it was strongly anti-Communist. It aimed to defend the free world, to encourage economic growth at home, and to ensure that the resulting plenty was fairly distributed. Their agenda much influenced by Keynesian economic theory-envisioned massive public expenditure that would speed economic growth, thus providing the public resources to fund larger welfare, housing, health, and educational programs.

Robert F. Kennedy and Martin Luther King, Jr., June 22, 1963, Washington, D.C.

Johnson was rewarded with an **electoral landslide in 1964** against conservative **Barry Goldwater**, which broke the decades-long control of Congress by the **Conservative coalition**. However, the Republicans bounced back in 1966 and elected **Richard Nixon** in 1968. Nixon largely continued the New Deal and Great Society programs he inherited; conservative reaction would come with the election of **Ronald Reagan** in 1980.Meanwhile, the American people completed a great migration from farms into the cities and experienced a period of sustained economic expansion.

Civil Rights Movement

African-American Civil Rights Movement (1955–68)

Duncan West speaking withCesar Chavez. The Delano **UFW**rally. Duncan represented the Teamsters who were supporting the UFW and condeming their IBT leadership for working as thugs against a fellow union. Duncan and his wife Mary were the branch organizers of the LA IS.

Starting in the late 1950s, institutionalized **racism across the United States**, but especially in the **South**, was increasingly challenged by the growing Civil Rights movement. The activism of African-American leaders **Rosa Parks** and **Martin Luther King, Jr.** led to the **Montgomery Bus Boycott**, which launched the movement. For years African Americans would struggle with violence against them but would achieve great steps toward equality with Supreme Court decisions, including *Brown v. Board of Education* and *Loving v. Virginia*, the **Civil Rights Act of 1964**, the **Voting Rights Act of 1965**, and the **Fair Housing Act of 1968**, which ended the **Jim Crow laws** that legalized **racial segregation** between whites and blacks.Martin Luther King, Jr., who had won the **Nobel Peace Prize** for his efforts to achieve equality of the races, was **assassinated in 1968**. Following his death others led the movement, most notably King's widow, **Coretta Scott King**, who was also active, like her husband, in the **Opposition to the Vietnam War**, and in the **Women's Liberation Movement**. There were 164 riots in 128 American cities in the first nine months of 1967. **Black Power** emerged during the late 1960s and early 1970s. The decade would ultimately bring about positive strides toward integration, especially in government service, sports, and entertainment. Native Americans turned to the federal courts to fight for their land rights. They held protests highlighting the federal government's failure to honor treaties. One of the most outspoken Native American groups was the American Indian Movement (AIM). In the 1960s, Cesar Chavez began organizing poorly paid Mexican-American farm workers in California. He led a five-year-long strike by grape pickers. Then Chávez formed the nation's first successful union of farm workers. His United Farm Workers of America (UFW) faltered after a few years but after Chavez died in 1993 he became an iconic "folk saint" in the pantheon of Mexican Americans.

The Women's Movement
Second-wave feminism

Gloria Steinem at a meeting of the Women's Action Alliance, 1972.

A new consciousness of the inequality of American women began sweeping the nation, starting with the 1963 publication of Betty Friedan's best-seller, *The Feminine Mystique*, which explained how many housewives felt trapped and unfulfilled, assaulted American culture for its creation of the notion that women could only find fulfillment through their roles as wives, mothers, and keepers of the home, and argued that women were just as able as men to do every type of job. In 1966 Friedan and others established the National Organization for Women, or NOW, to act for women as the NAACP did for African Americans.

Protests began, and the new Women's Liberation Movement grew in size and power, gained much media attention, and, by 1968, had replaced the Civil Rights Movement as the US's main social revolution. Marches, parades, rallies, boycotts, and pickets brought out thousands, sometimes millions. There were striking gains for women in medicine, law, and business, while only a few were elected to office. The Movement was split into factions by political ideology early on, however (with NOW on the left, the Women's Equity Action League (WEAL) on the right, the National Women's Political Caucus (NWPC) in the center, and more radical groups formed by younger women on the far left). The proposed Equal Rights Amendment to the Constitution, passed by Congress in 1972 was defeated by a conservative coalition mobilized by Phyllis Schlafly. They argued that it degraded the position of the housewife and made young women susceptible to the military draft.

However, many federal laws (i.e., those equalizing pay, employment, education, employment opportunities, and credit; ending pregnancy discrimination; and requiring NASA, the Military Academies, and other organizations to admit women), state laws (i.e., those ending spousal abuse and marital rape), Supreme Court rulings (i.e. ruling that the equal protection clause of the Fourteenth Amendment applied to women), and state ERAs established women's equal status under the law, and social custom and consciousness began to change, accepting women's equality. The controversial issue of abortion, deemed by the Supreme Court as a fundamental right in *Roe v. Wade* (1973), is still a point of debate today.

The Counterculture Revolution and Cold War Détente
History of the United States (1964–80)

Amid the Cold War, the United States entered the Vietnam War, whose growing unpopularity fed already existing social movements, including those among women, minorities, and young people. President Lyndon B. Johnson's Great Society social programs and numerous rulings by the Warren Court added to the wide range of social reform during the 1960s and 1970s. Feminism and the environmental movement became political forces, and progress continued toward civil rights for all Americans. The Counterculture Revolution swept through the nation and much of the western world in the late sixties and early seventies, further dividing Americans in a "culture war" but also bringing forth more liberated social views.

United States Navy **F-4 Phantom II**shadows a Soviet **Tu-95 Bear** D aircraft in the early 1970s

Johnson was succeeded in 1969 by Republican **Richard Nixon**, who **attempted to gradually turn the war over to** the **South Vietnamese** forces.; He negotiated the **peace treaty in 1973** which secured the release of POWs and lead to the withdrawal of U.S. troops. The war had cost the lives of 58,000 American troops. Nixon manipulated the fierce distrust between the Soviet Union and China to the advantage of the United States, achieving *détente* (relaxation; ease of tension) with both parties.

The **Watergate scandal**, involving Nixon's cover-up of his operatives' break-in into the **Democratic National Committee** headquarters at the**Watergate office complex** destroyed his political base, sent many aides to prison, and forced Nixon's resignation on August 9, 1974. He was succeeded by Vice President **Gerald Ford**. The **Fall of Saigon** ended the Vietnam War and resulted in North and South **Vietnam** being reunited. Communist victories in neighboring **Cambodia** and **Laos** occurred in the same year.

The **OPEC oil embargo** marked a long-term economic transition since, for the first time, energy prices skyrocketed, and American factories faced serious competition from foreign automobiles, clothing, electronics, and consumer goods. By the late 1970s the economy suffered an**energy crisis**, slow economic growth, high unemployment, and very high inflation coupled with high interest rates (the term **stagflation** was coined). Since economists agreed on the wisdom of **deregulation**, many of the New Deal era regulations were ended, such as in transportation, banking, and telecommunications.

Jimmy Carter, running as someone who was not a part of the Washington political establishment, was elected president in 1976. On the world stage, Carter brokered the **Camp David Accords** between Israel and Egypt. In 1979, Iranian students stormed the US embassy in **Tehran** and took 66 Americans hostage, resulting in the Iran hostage crisis. With the hostage crisis and continuing stagflation, Carter lost the 1980 election to the Republican Ronald Reagan. On January 20, 1981, minutes after Carter's term in office ended, the remaining U.S. captives held at the U.S. embassy in Iran were released, ending the 444-day hostage crisis.

Close of the 20th century

History of the United States (1980–91)

Ronald Reagan at the Brandenburg Gate challenges Soviet premier Mikhail Gorbachev to tear down the Berlin Wallin 1987, shortly before the end of theCold War

Ronald Reagan produced a major realignment with his 1980 and 1984 landslide elections. Reagan's economic policies (dubbed "Reaganomics") and the implementation of the Economic Recovery Tax Act of 1981 lowered income taxes from 70% to 28% over the course of seven years. Reagan continued to downsize government taxation and regulation. The US experienced a recession in 1982, but the negative indicators reversed, with the inflation rate decreasing from 11% to 2%, the unemployment rate decreasing from 10.8% in December 1982 to 7.5% in November 1984, and the economic growth rate increasing from 4.5% to 7.2%.

Reagan ordered a buildup of the US military, incurring additional budget deficits. Reagan introduced a complicated missile defense system known as the Strategic Defense Initiative (SDI) (dubbed "Star Wars" by opponents) in which, theoretically, the U.S. could shoot down missiles with laser systems in space. The Soviets reacted harshly because they thought it violated the 1972 Anti-Ballistic Missile Treaty, and would upset the balance of power by giving the U.S. a major military advantage. For years, Soviet leader Mikhail Gorbachev argued vehemently against SDI. However, by the late 1980s he decided the system would never work and should not be used to block disarmament deals with the

U.S.Historians argue how great an impact the SDI threat had on the Soviets – whether it was enough to force Gorbachev to initiate radical reforms, or whether the deterioration of the Soviet economy alone forced the reforms. There is agreement that the Soviets realized they were well behind the Americans in military technology, that to try to catch up would be very expensive, and that the military expenses were already a very heavy burden slowing down their economy.

Reagan's Invasion of Grenada and bombing of Libya were popular in the US, though his backing of the Contras rebels was mired in the controversy over the Iran–Contra affair that revealed Reagan's poor management style.

Reagan met four times with Soviet leader Mikhail Gorbachev, who ascended to power in 1985, and their summit conferences led to the signing of the Intermediate-Range Nuclear Forces Treaty. Gorbachev tried to save Communism in the Soviet Union first by ending the expensive arms race with America. Then by shedding the East European empire in 1989. The Soviet Union collapsed on Christmas Day 1991, ending the US–Soviet Cold War.

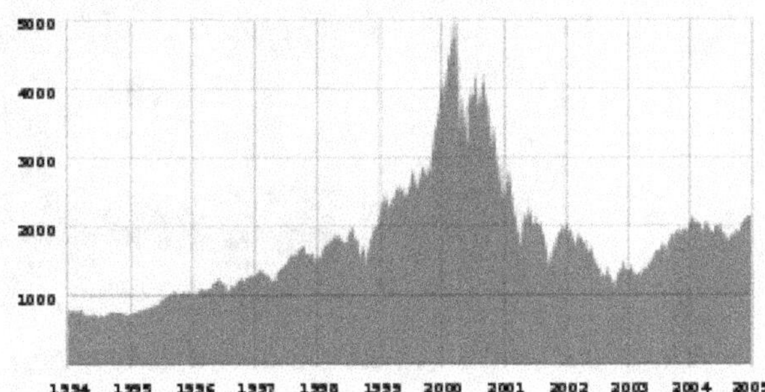

The NASDAQ Composite index swelled with the dot-com bubble in the optimistic "New Economy". The bubble burst in 2000.

The United States emerged as the world's sole remaining superpower and continued to intervene in international affairs during the 1990s, including the 1991 Gulf War against Iraq. Following his election in 1992, President Bill Clinton oversaw one of the longest periods of economic expansion and unprecedented gains in securities values, a side effect of the digital revolution and new business opportunities created by the Internet. He also worked with the Republican Congress to pass the first balanced federal budget in 30 years.

In 1998, Clinton was impeached by the House of Representatives on charges of "high crimes and misdemeanors" for lying about a sexual relationship with White House intern Monica Lewinsky but was later acquitted by the Senate. The failure of impeachment and the Democratic gains in the 1998 election forced House Speaker Newt Gingrich, a Republican, to resign from Congress.

The presidential election in 2000 between George W. Bush and Al Gore was one of the closest in US history and helped lay the seeds for political polarization to come. The vote in the decisive state of Florida was extremely close and produced a dramatic dispute over the counting of votes. The US Supreme Court in *Bush v. Gore* ended the recount with a 5–4 vote. That meant Bush, then in the lead, carried Florida and the election.

21st century

History of the United States (1991–present)

9/11 and the War on Terror
September 11 attacks, *War on Terror* and *Nuclear 9/11*

The September 11 attacks led to the War on Terror.

On September 11, 2001 ("9/11"), the United States was struck by a terrorist attack when 19 al-Qaeda hijackers commandeered four airliners and intentionally crashed into both twin towers of the World Trade Center and into the Pentagon, killing 2,550 American civilians and 55 military personnel, along with 372 non-Americans (excluding the 19 hijackers). The fourth plane, United flight 93, was re-taken by the passengers and crew of the aircraft. While they were not able to land the plane safely, they were able to re-take control of the aircraft and crash it into an empty field in Pennsylvania, thereby saving whatever target the terrorists were aiming for. In response on September 20, President George W. Bush announced a "War on Terror". On October 7, 2001, the United States and NATO then invaded Afghanistan to oust the Taliban regime, which had provided safe haven to al-Qaeda and its leader Osama bin Laden.

The federal government established new domestic efforts to prevent future attacks. The controversial USA PATRIOT Act increased the government's power to monitor communications and removed legal restrictions on information sharing between federal law enforcement and intelligence services. A cabinet-level agency called the Department of Homeland Security was created to lead and coordinate federal counter-terrorism activities. Some of these anti-terrorism efforts, particularly the US government's handling of detainees at the prison at Guantanamo Bay, led to allegations against the US government of human rights violations.

In 2003, from March 19 to May 1, the United States launched an invasion of Iraq, which led to the collapse of the Iraq government and the eventual capture of Iraqi dictator Saddam Hussein, with whom the US had long-standing tense relations. The reasons for the invasion cited by the Bush administration included the spreading of democracy, the elimination of weapons of mass destruction (a key demand of the UN as well, though later investigations found parts of the intelligence reports to be inaccurate), and the liberation of the Iraqi people. Despite some initial successes early in the invasion, the continued Iraq War fueled international protests and gradually saw domestic support decline as many people began to question whether or not the invasion was worth the cost. In 2007, after years of violence by the Iraqi insurgency, President Bush deployed more troops in a strategy dubbed "the surge". While the death toll decreased, the political stability of Iraq remained in doubt.

In 2008, the unpopularity of President Bush and the Iraq war, along with the 2008 financial crisis, led to the election of Barack Obama, the first African-American President of the United States. After his election, Obama reluctantly continued the war effort in Iraq until August 31, 2010, when he declared that combat operations had ended. However, 50,000 American soldiers and military personnel were kept in Iraq to assist Iraqi forces, help protect withdrawing forces, and work on counter-terrorism until December 15, 2011, when the war was declared formally over and the last troops left the country. At the same time, Obama increased American involvement in Afghanistan, starting a surge strategy using an additional 30,000 troops, while proposing to begin withdrawing troops sometime in December 2014. With regards to Guantanamo Bay, President Obama forbade torture but in general retained Bush's policy regarding the Guantanamo detainees, while also proposing that the prison eventually be closed.

In May 2011, after nearly a decade in hiding, the founder and leader of Al Qaeda, Osama bin Laden, was killed in Pakistan in a raid conducted by US naval special forces acting under President Obama's direct orders. While Al Qaeda was near collapse in Afghanistan, affiliated organizations continued to operate in Yemen and other remote areas as the CIA useddrones to hunt down and remove its leadership.

The Islamic State of Iraq and the Levant - formerly known as Al-Qaeda in Iraq - rose to prominence in September 2014. In addition to taking control of much of Western Iraq and Eastern Syria, ISIS also beheaded three journalists, two American and one British. These events lead to a major military offensive by the USA and its allies in the region.

On December 28, 2014, President Obama officially ended the combat mission in Afghanistan and promised a withdraw of all remaining troops at the end of 2016 with the exception of the embassy guards.

The Great Recession

Great Recession

Lehman Brothers(headquarters pictured) filed for bankruptcy in September 2008 at the height of the U.S.financial crisis.

In September 2008, the United States, and most of Europe, entered the longest post–World War II recession, often called the "Great Recession." Multiple overlapping crises were involved, especially the housing market crisis, a subprime mortgage crisis, soaring oil prices, anautomotive industry crisis, rising unemployment, and the worst financial crisis since the Great Depression. The financial crisis threatened the stability of the entire economy in September 2008 when Lehman Brothers failed and other giant banks were in grave danger.Starting in October the federal government lent $245 billion to financial institutions through the Troubled Asset Relief Program which was passed by bipartisan majorities and signed by Bush.

Following his election victory by a wide electoral margin in November 2008, Bush's successor - Barack Obama - signed into law the American Recovery and Reinvestment Act of 2009, which was a $787 billion economic stimulus aimed at helping the economy recover from the deepening recession. Obama, like Bush, took steps to rescue the auto industry and prevent future economic meltdowns. These included a bailout of General Motors andChrysler, putting ownership temporarily in the hands of the government, and the "cash for clunkers" program which temporarily boosted new car sales.

The recession officially ended in June 2009, and the economy slowly began to expand once again The unemployment rate peaked at 10.1% in October 2009 after surging from 4.7% in November 2007, and gradually fell to 6.2% as of July 2014. However, overall economic growth has remained weaker in the 2010s compared to expansions in previous decades.

Recent events

President Barack Obama signs thePatient Protection and Affordable Care Act.

From 2009 to 2010, the 111th Congress passed major legislation such as the Patient Protection and Affordable Care Act, the Dodd-Frank Wall Street Reform and Consumer Protection Act and the Don't Ask, Don't Tell Repeal Act, which were signed into law by President Obama.Following the 2010 midterm elections, which resulted in a Republican-controlled House of Representatives and a Democratic-controlled Senate,Congress presided over a period of elevated gridlock and heated debates over whether or not raise the debt ceiling, extend tax cuts for citizens making over $250,000 annually, and many other key issues. These ongoing debates led to

President Obama signing the Budget Control Act of 2011. In the Fall of 2012, Mitt Romney challenged Barack Obama. Following Obama's reelection in November 2012, Congress passed the American Taxpayer Relief Act of 2012 - which resulted in an increase in taxes primarily on those earning the most money. Congressional gridlock continued as Congressional Republicans' call for the repeal of the Patient Protection and Affordable Care Act - popularly known as "Obamacare" - along with other various demands, resulted in the first government shutdown since the Clinton administration and almost led to the first default on U.S. debt since the 19th century. As a result of growing public frustration with both parties in Congress since the beginning of the decade, Congressional approval ratings fell to record lows, with only 11% of Americans approving as of October 2013.

Other major events that have occurred during the 2010s include the rise of new political movements, such as the conservative Tea Party movement and the liberal Occupy movement. There was also unusually severe weather during the early part of the decade. In 2012, over half the country experienced record drought and Hurricane Sandy caused massive damage to coastal areas of New York and New Jersey.

The ongoing debate over the issue of rights for the LGBT community, most notably that of same-sex marriage, began to shift in favor of same-sex couples, and has been reflected in dozens of polls released in the early part of the decade. In 2012, President Obama becoming the first president to openly support same-sex marriage, and the 2013 Supreme Court decision in the case of United States v. Windsor provided for federal recognition of same-sex unions.

As of 2015, political debate has continued over issues such as tax reform, immigration reform, income inequality and US foreign policy in the Middle East, particularly with regards to global terrorism and the rise of the Islamic State in Iraq and the Levant.

Geography, climate, and environment

Geography of the United States, *Climate of the United States* and *Environment of the United States*

A composite satellite image of the contiguous United States and surrounding areas

The land area of the contiguous United States is 2,959,064 square miles (7.7 Mm²). Alaska, separated from the contiguous United States by Canada, is the largest state at 663,268 square miles (1.7 Mm²). Hawaii, occupying an archipelago in the central Pacific, southwest of North America, is 10,931 square miles (28,311 km²) in area.

The United States is the world's third or fourth largest nation by total area (land and water), ranking behind Russia and Canada and just above or below China. The ranking varies depending on how two territories disputed by China and India are counted and how the total size of the United States is measured: calculations range from 3,676,486 square miles (9.5 Mm²) to 3,717,813 square miles (9.6 Mm²) to 3,794,101 square miles (9.8 Mm²). to 3,805,927 square miles (9.9 Mm²). Measured by only land area, the United States is third in size behind Russia and China, just ahead of Canada.

The coastal plain of the Atlantic seaboard gives way further inland to deciduous forests and the rolling hills of the Piedmont. TheAppalachian Mountains divide the eastern seaboard from the Great Lakes and the grasslands of the Midwest. The Mississippi–Missouri River, the world's fourth longest river system, runs mainly north–south through the heart of the country. The flat, fertile prairie of the Great Plains stretches to the west, interrupted by a highland region in the southeast.

The Rocky Mountains, at the western edge of the Great Plains, extend north to south across the country, reaching altitudes higher than 14,000 feet (4.3 km) in Colorado. Further west are the rocky Great Basin and deserts such as the Chihuahua and Mojave.The Sierra Nevada and Cascade mountain ranges run close to the Pacific coast, both ranges reaching altitudes higher than 14,000 feet (4.3 km). The lowest and highest points in the continental United States are in the state of California, and only about 84 miles (135 km) apart. At 20,320 feet (6.2 km), Alaska's Mount McKinley is the tallest peak in the country and in North America. Active volcanoes are common throughout

Alaska's [Alexander](#)and [Aleutian Islands](#), and Hawaii consists of volcanic islands. The [supervolcano](#) underlying [Yellowstone National Park](#) in the Rockies is the continent's largest volcanic feature.The United States, with its large size and geographic variety, includes most climate types. To the east of the [100th meridian](#), the climate ranges from [humid continental](#) in the north to[humid subtropical](#) in the south. The southern tip of [Florida](#) is tropical, as is Hawaii The Great Plains west of the 100th meridian are semi-arid. Much of the Western mountains have an [alpine climate](#). The climate is arid in the Great Basin, desert in the Southwest, [Mediterranean](#) in [coastal California](#), and [oceanic](#) in coastal [Oregon](#) and [Washington](#) and southern Alaska. Most of Alaska is subarctic or polar. Extreme weather is not uncommon—the states bordering the [Gulf of Mexico](#) are prone to [hurricanes](#), and most of the world's[tornadoes](#) occur within the country, mainly in [Tornado Alley](#) areas in the Midwest.

Wildlife

[*Fauna of the United States*](#) and [*Flora of the United States*](#)

The [bald eagle](#) has been the national bird of the United States since 1782.

The U.S. ecology is [megadiverse](#): about 17,000 species of [vascular plants](#) occur in the contiguous United States and Alaska, and over 1,800 species of[flowering plants](#) are found in Hawaii, few of which occur on the mainland. The United States is home to 428 mammal species, 784 bird species, 311 reptile species, and 295 amphibian species. About 91,000 insect species have been described. The [bald eagle](#) is both the [national bird](#) and[national animal](#) of the United States, and is an enduring symbol of the country itself.There are 58 [national parks](#) and hundreds of other federally managed parks, forests, and [wilderness](#) areas. Altogether, the government owns about 28% of the country's land area. Most of this is [protected](#), though some is leased for oil and gas drilling, mining, logging, or cattle ranching; about .86% is used for military purposes.<u>Environmental issues</u> have been on the national agenda since 1970. Environmental controversies include debates on oil and <u>nuclear energy</u>, dealing with air and water pollution, the economic costs of protecting wildlife, logging and <u>deforestation</u>, and international responses to global warming. Many federal and state agencies are involved. The most prominent is the <u>Environmental Protection Agency</u> (EPA), created by presidential order in 1970. The idea of wilderness has shaped the management of public lands since 1964, with the Wilderness Act.The<u>Endangered Species Act</u> of 1973 is intended to protect threatened and endangered species and their habitats, which are monitored by the <u>United States Fish and Wildlife Service</u>.

Demographics

<u>*Demographics of the United States*</u>, <u>*Americans*</u>, <u>*List of U.S. states by population density*</u> and <u>*List of United States cities by population*</u>

Population

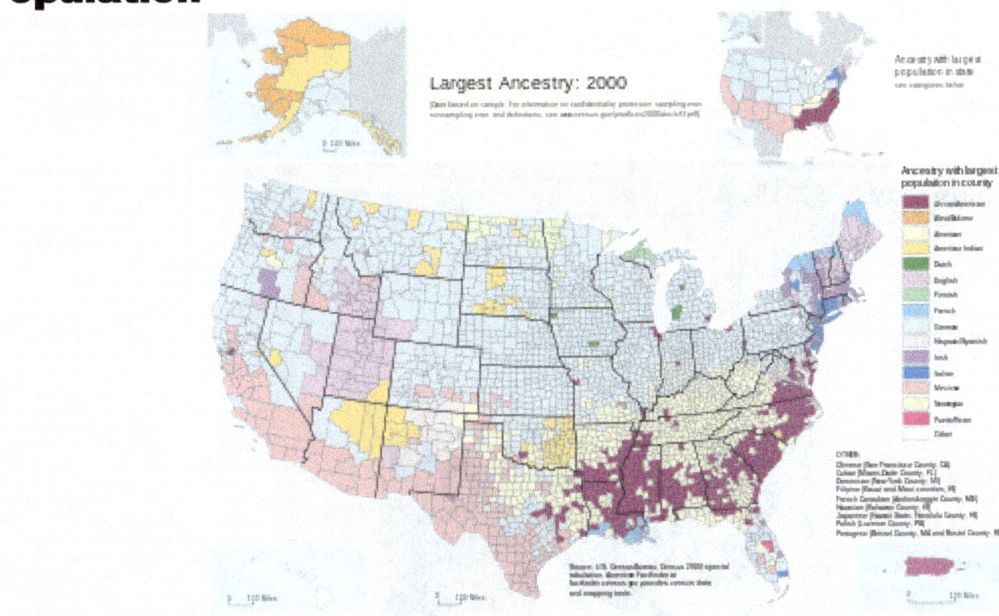

Largest ancestry groups by county, 2000

Race/Ethnicity (2013)

By race:[190]

White	**77.7%**
African American	**13.2%**
Asian	**5.3%**
American Indian and **Alaska Native**	**1.2%**
Native Hawaiian and **Pacific Islander**	**0.2%**
Multiracial (2 or more)	**2.4%**
By ethnicity:	
Hispanic/Latino (of any race)	**17.1%**
Non-Hispanic/Latino (of any race)	**82.9%**

The **Statue of Liberty** in **New York City** is a symbol of both the U.S. and the ideals of freedom, democracy, and opportunity.

The **U.S. Census Bureau** estimates the country's population now to be 320,657,000, The U.S. population almost quadrupled during the 20th century, from about 76 million in 1900. The third most populous nation in the world, after

China and India, the United States is the only major industrialized nation in which large population increases are projected.

The United States has a very diverse population; 37 ancestry groups have more than one million members.German Americans are the largest ethnic group (more than 50 million) - followed by Irish Americans (circa 37 million), Mexican Americans (circa 31 million) and English Americans (circa 28 million).

White Americans are the largest racial group; Black Americans are the nation's largest racial minority and third largest ancestry group. Asian Americans are the country's second largest racial minority; the three largest Asian American ethnic groups are Chinese Americans, Filipino Americans, and Indian Americans.

The United States has a birth rate of 13 per 1,000, which is 5 births below the world average. Its population growth rate is positive at 0.7%, higher than that of many developed nations. In fiscal year 2012, over one million immigrants (most of whom entered through family reunification) were granted legal residence. Mexicohas been the leading source of new residents since the 1965 Immigration Act. China, India, and the Philippineshave been in the top four sending countries every year since the 1990s. As of 2012, approximately 11.4 million residents are illegal immigrants.According to a survey conducted by the Williams Institute, nine million Americans, or roughly 3.4% of the adult population identify themselves as homosexual, bisexual, or transgender. A 2012 Gallup poll also concluded that 3.5% of adult Americans identified as LGBT. The highest percentage came from the District of Columbia (10%), while the lowest state was North Dakota at 1.7%. In a 2013 survey, theCenters for Disease Control and Prevention found that 96.6% of Americans identify as straight, while 1.6% identify as gay or lesbian, and 0.7% identify as being bisexual.

In 2010, the U.S. population included an estimated 5.2 million people with some American Indian or Alaska Native ancestry (2.9 million exclusively of such ancestry) and 1.2 million with some native Hawaiian or Pacific island ancestry (0.5 million exclusively). The census counted more than 19 million people of "Some Other Race" who were "unable to identify with any" of its five official race categories in 2010.

The population growth of Hispanic and Latino Americans (the terms are officially interchangeable) is a major demographic trend. The 50.5 million Americans of Hispanic descent are identified as sharing a distinct "ethnicity" by the Census Bureau; 64% of Hispanic Americans are of Mexican descent. Between 2000 and 2010, the country's Hispanic population increased 43% while the non-Hispanic population rose just 4.9%. Much of this growth is from immigration; in 2007, 12.6% of the U.S. population was foreign-born, with 54% of that figure born in Latin America.

Fertility is also a factor; in 2010 the average Hispanic (of any race) woman gave birth to 2.35 children in her lifetime, compared to 1.97 for non-Hispanic black women and 1.79 for non-Hispanic white women (both below the replacement rate of 2.1). Minorities (as defined by the Census Bureau as all those beside non-Hispanic, non-multiracial whites) constituted 36.3% of the population in 2010, and over 50% of children under age one, and are projected to constitute the majority by 2042.This contradicts the report by the National Vital Statistics Reports, based on the U.S. census data, which concludes that 54% (2,162,406 out of 3,999,386 in 2010) of births were non-Hispanic white.

About 82% of Americans live in urban areas (including suburbs); about half of those reside in cities with populations over 50,000. In 2008, 273 incorporated places had populations over 100,000, nine cities had more than one million residents, and four global cities had over two million (New York City, Los Angeles, Chicago, and Houston). There are 52 metropolitan areas with populations greater than one million.Of the 50 fastest-growing metro areas, 47 are in the West or South. The metro areas of San Bernardino, Dallas, Houston, Atlanta, andPhoenix all grew by more than a million people between 2000 and 2008.

Languages spoken at home by more than 1,000,000 persons in the U.S. as of 2010

Language	Percent of population	Number of speakers
English (only)	80%	233,780,338
Combined total of all languages other than English	*20%*	*57,048,617*

Spanish (excluding **Puerto Rico** and **Spanish Creole**)	**12%**	**35,437,985**
Chinese (including **Cantonese** and **Mandarin**)	**0.9%**	**2,567,779**
Tagalog	**0.5%**	**1,542,118**
Vietnamese	**0.4%**	**1,292,448**
French	**0.4%**	**1,288,833**
Korean	**0.4%**	**1,108,408**
German	**0.4%**	**1,107,869**

Language

Languages of the United States

Language Spoken at Home in the United States of America and *List of endangered languages in the United States*

English (American English) is the de facto national language. Although there is no official language at the federal level, some laws—such as U.S. naturalization requirements—standardize English. In 2010, about 230 million, or 80% of the population aged five years and older, spoke only English at home. Spanish, spoken by 12% of the population at home, is the second most common language and the most widely taught second language.Some Americans advocate making English the country's official language, as it is in 28 states.

Both Hawaiian and English are official languages in Hawaii, by state law, Alaska recognizes many Native languages. While neither has an official language, New Mexico has laws providing for the use of both English and Spanish, as [Louisiana](#) does for English and [French](#). Other states, such as [California](#), mandate the publication of Spanish versions of certain government documents including court forms. Many jurisdictions with large numbers of non-English speakers produce government materials, especially voting information, in the most commonly spoken languages in those jurisdictions.

Several insular territories grant official recognition to their native languages, along with English: [Samoan](#) and[Chamorro](#)are recognized by American Samoa and Guam, respectively; [Carolinian](#) and Chamorro are recognized by the Northern Mariana Islands; [Cherokee](#) is officially recognized by the [Cherokee Nation](#) within the Cherokee tribal jurisdiction area in eastern Oklahoma;[228] Spanish is an official language of [Puerto Rico](#) and is more widely spoken than English there.[229]

Religion

[Religion in the United States](#)

[History of religion in the United States](#), *[Freedom of religion in the United States](#)*, *[Separation of church and state in the United States](#)* and *[List of religious movements that began in the United States](#)*

Religious affiliation in the U.S. (2007)

Affiliation	% of U.S. population	
[Christian](#)	79	
[Evangelical Protestant](#)	26	
[Catholic](#)	24	
[Mainline Protestant](#)	18	
[Black Protestant](#)	7	

Religious affiliation in the U.S. (2007)

Affiliation	% of U.S. population	
Mormon	1.7	
Other Christian	1.6	
Judaism	1.7	
Buddhism	0.7	
Islam	0.6	
Hinduism	0.4	
Other faith	1.2	
Unaffiliated	16	
Don't know/refused answer	0.8	
Total	100	

The First Amendment of the U.S. Constitution guarantees the free exercise of religion and forbids Congress from passing laws respecting its establishment. Christianity is by far the most common religion practiced in the U.S., but other religions are followed, too. In a 2013 survey, 56% of Americans said that religion played a "very important role in their lives", a far higher figure than that of any other wealthy nation. In a 2009 Gallup poll 42% of Americans said that they attended church weekly or almost weekly; the figures ranged from a low of 23% in Vermont to a high of 63% in Mississippi.As with other Western countries, the U.S. is becoming less religious. Irreligion is growing rapidly among Americans under 30. Polls show that overall American confidence in organized religion is declining, and that younger Americans in particular are becoming increasingly irreligious.

According to a 2014 survey, 78.5% of adults identified themselves as Christian,Protestant denominations accounted for 51.3%, while Roman Catholicism, at 23.9%, was the largest individual denomination. The total reporting non-Christian religions in 2012 was 4.9%, up from 4% in 2007.[237] Other religions include Judaism(1.7%), Buddhism (0.7%), Islam (0.6%), Hinduism (0.4%), and Unitarian Universalism (0.3%). The survey also reported that 16.1% of Americans described themselves as agnostic, atheist or simply having no religion, up from 8.2% in 1990.There are also Baha'i, Sikh, Jain, Shinto, Confucian, Taoist, Druid, Native American, Wiccan, humanist and deist communities.Protestantism is the largest Christian religious grouping in the United States. Baptists collectively form the largest branch of Protestantism, and the Southern Baptist Convention is the largest individual Protestant denomination. About 26 percent of Americans identify as Evangelical Protestants, while 18 percent are Mainline and 7 percent belong to a traditionally Black church. Roman Catholicism in the United States has its origin in the Spanish andFrench colonization of the Americas, and later grew due to Irish, Italian, Polish, German and Hispanic immigration. Rhode Island is the only state where a majority of the population is Catholic. Lutheranism in the U.S. has its origin in immigration from Northern Europe. North and South Dakota are the only states in which a plurality of the population is Lutheran. Utah is the only state whereMormonism is the religion of the majority of the population. The Mormon Corridor also extends to parts of Idaho, Nevada and Wyoming. The Bible Belt is an informal term for a region in the Southern United States in which socially conservative Evangelical Protestantism is a significant part of the culture and Christian church attendance across the denominations is generally higher than the nation's average. By contrast, religion plays the least important role in New England and in the Western United States.

Family structure

In 2007, 58% of Americans age 18 and over were married, 6% were widowed, 10% were divorced, and 25% had never been married Women now work mostly outside the home and receive a majority of bachelor's degrees.

The U.S. teenage pregnancy rate, 79.8 per 1,000 women, is the highest among OECD nations. Between 2007 and 2010, the highest teenage birth rate was in Mississippi, and the lowest in New Hampshire. Abortion is legal throughout the U.S., owing to *Roe v. Wade*, a 1973 landmark decision by the Supreme Court of the United States. While the abortion rate is falling, the abortion ratio of 241 per 1,000 live births and abortion rate of 15 per 1,000 women aged 15–44 remain higher than those of most Western nations. In 2011, the average age at first birth was 25.6 and 40.7% of births were to unmarried women. The total fertility rate (TFR) was estimated for 2013 at 1.86 births per woman. Adoption in the United States is common and relatively easy from a legal point of view (compared to other Western countries). In 2001, with over 127,000 adoptions, the U.S. accounted for nearly half of the total number of adoptions worldwide.The legal status of same-sex couples adopting varies by jurisdiction. Polygamy is illegal throughout the U.S.

Government and politics

The United States Capitol,
where Congress meets:
the Senate, left; the House, right

The White House, home of the U.S. President

[Supreme Court Building](#), where the[nation's highest court](#)sits

The United States is the world's oldest surviving [federation](#). It is a [constitutional republic](#) and[representative democracy](#), "in which [majority rule](#) is tempered by [minority rights](#) protected by [law](#)".[252]The government is regulated by a system of [checks and balances](#) defined by the U.S. Constitution, which serves as the country's supreme legal document.[253] For 2013, the U.S. ranked 19th on the [Democracy Index](#)[254] and 17th on the [Corruption Perceptions Index](#).[255]

In the [American federalist system](#), citizens are usually subject to [three levels of government](#): federal, state, and local. The [local government](#)'s duties are commonly split between [county](#) and [municipal governments](#). In almost all cases, executive and legislative officials are elected by a [plurality vote](#) of citizens by district. There is no [proportional representation](#) at the federal level, and it is very rare at lower levels.

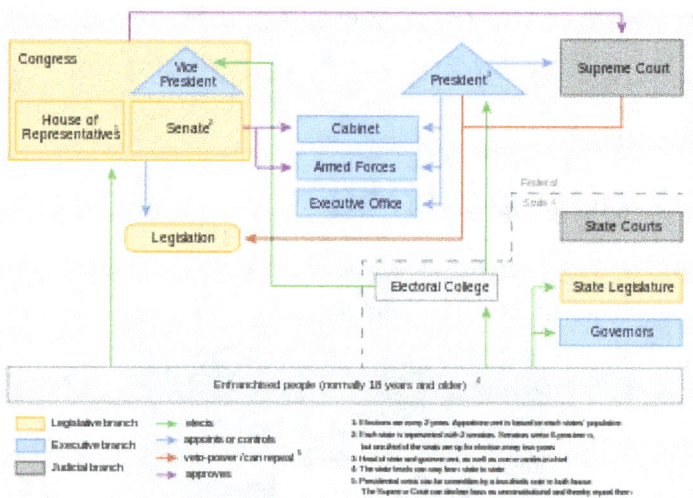

Political system of the United States

The federal government is composed of three branches:

- [Legislative](#): The [bicameral](#) [Congress](#), made up of the [Senate](#) and the [House of Representatives](#), makes [federal law](#),[declares war](#), approves treaties, has the [power of the purse](#), and has the power of [impeachment](#), by which it can remove sitting members of the government.

- **Executive**: The President is the commander-in-chief of the military, can veto legislative bills before they become law (subject to Congressional override), and appoints the members of the Cabinet (subject to Senate approval) and other officers, who administer and enforce federal laws and policies.
- **Judicial**: The Supreme Court and lower federal courts, whose judges are appointed by the President with Senate approval, interpret laws and overturn those they find unconstitutional.

The House of Representatives has 435 voting members, each representing a congressional district for a two-year term. House seats are apportioned among the states by population every tenth year. At the 2010 census, seven states had the minimum of one representative, while California, the most populous state, had 53.

The Senate has 100 members with each state having two senators, elected at-large to six-year terms; one third of Senate seats are up for election every other year. The President serves a four-year term and may be elected to the office no more than twice. The President is not elected by direct vote, but by an indirect electoral college system in which the determining votes are apportioned to the states and the District of Columbia. The Supreme Court, led by the Chief Justice of the United States, has nine members, who serve for life.

The state governments are structured in roughly similar fashion; Nebraska uniquely has a unicameral legislature. The governor (chief executive) of each state is directly elected. Some state judges and cabinet officers are appointed by the governors of the respective states, while others are elected by popular vote.

The original text of the Constitution establishes the structure and responsibilities of the federal government and its relationship with the individual states. Article One protects the right to the "great writ" of habeas corpus. The Constitution has been amended 27 times; the first ten amendments, which make up the Bill of Rights, and the Fourteenth Amendmentform the central basis of Americans' individual rights. All laws and governmental procedures are subject to judicial review and any law ruled by the courts to be in violation of the Constitution is voided. The principle of judicial review, not explicitly mentioned in the Constitution, was established by the Supreme Court in *Marbury v. Madison* (1803) in a decision handed down by Chief Justice John Marshall.

Political divisions

17 positions (four national candidates of the two major party in the [2012 presidential election](), four leaders in [112th United States Congress](), and nine [Supreme Court Justices]()) there is only one WASP.

The [United Nations Headquarters]()has been situated in [Midtown Manhattan]() since 1952.

Foreign relations

[Foreign relations of the United States]() and [Foreign policy of the United States]()

[Covert United States foreign regime change actions]()

The United States has an established structure of foreign relations. It is a permanent member of the [United Nations Security Council](), and New York City is home to the [United Nations Headquarters](). It is a member of the [G7](), [G20](), and [Organisation for Economic Co-operation and Development](). Almost all countries have [embassies]() in Washington, D.C., and many have [consulates]() around the country. Likewise, nearly all nations host [American diplomatic missions](). However, [Cuba](), [Iran](), [North Korea](), [Bhutan](), and the [Republic of China]() (Taiwan) do not have formal diplomatic relations with the United States (although the U.S. still supplies Taiwan with [military equipment]()).The United States has a "[special relationship]()" with the [United Kingdom]() and strong ties with [Canada](), [Australia](), [New Zealand](), [the Philippines](), [Japan](),[South Korea](), [Israel](), and several [European Union]() countries, including [France](), [Italy](), [Germany](), and [Spain](). It works closely with fellow [NATO]() members on military and security issues and with its neighbors through the [Organization of American States]()and [free trade agreements]() such as the trilateral [North American Free Trade Agreement]() with Canada and [Mexico](). In

2008, the United States spent a net $25.4 billion on official development assistance, the most in the world. As a share of America's large gross national income (GNI), however, the U.S. contribution of 0.18% ranked last among 22 donor states. By contrast, private overseas giving by Americans is relatively generous.

The U.S. exercises full international defense authority and responsibility for three sovereign nations through Compact of Free Association withMicronesia, the Marshall Islands and Palau, all of which are Pacific island nations which were part of the U.S.-administered Trust Territory of the Pacific Islands beginning after World War II, and gained independence in subsequent years.

Government finance

Taxation in the United States and *United States federal budget*

Taxes are levied in the United States at the federal, state and local government level. These include taxes on income, payroll, property, sales, imports, estates and gifts, as well as various fees. In 2010 taxes collected by federal, state and municipal governments amounted to 24.8% of GDP. During FY2012, the federal government collected approximately $2.45 trillion in tax revenue, up $147 billion or 6% versus FY2011 revenues of $2.30 trillion. Primary receipt categories included individual income taxes ($1,132B or 47%), Social Security/Social Insurance taxes ($845B or 35%), and corporate taxes ($242B or 10%).

U.S. taxation is generally progressive, especially the federal income taxes, and is among the most progressive in the developed world,[297] but the incidence of corporate income taxhas been a matter of considerable ongoing controversy for decades. In 2009 the top 10% of earners, with 36% of the nation's income, paid 78.2% of the federal personal income tax burden, while the bottom 40% had a negative liability.However, payroll taxes for Social Security are a flat regressive tax, with no tax charged on income above $113,700 and no tax at all paid on unearned income from things such as stocks and capital gains. The historic reasoning for the regressive nature of the payroll tax is that entitlement programs have not been viewed as welfare transfers. The top 10% paid 51.8% of total federal taxes in 2009, and the top 1%, with 13.4% of pre-tax national income, paid 22.3% of federal taxes.In 2013 the Tax Policy Center projected total federal effective tax rates of 35.5% for the top 1%, 27.2% for the top quintile, 13.8% for the middle quintile, and −2.7% for the bottom quintile. State and local taxes vary widely, but are generally less progressive than federal taxes as they rely heavily on broadly borne[regressive](#) sales and property taxes that yield less volatile revenue streams, though their consideration does not eliminate the progressive nature of overall taxation.

During FY 2012, the federal government spent $3.54 trillion on a budget or cash basis, down $60 billion or 1.7% vs. FY 2011 spending of $3.60 trillion. Major categories of FY 2012 spending included: Medicare & Medicaid ($802B or 23% of spending), Social Security ($768B or 22%), Defense Department ($670B or 19%), non-defense discretionary ($615B or 17%), other mandatory ($461B or 13%) and interest ($223B or 6%).

National debt

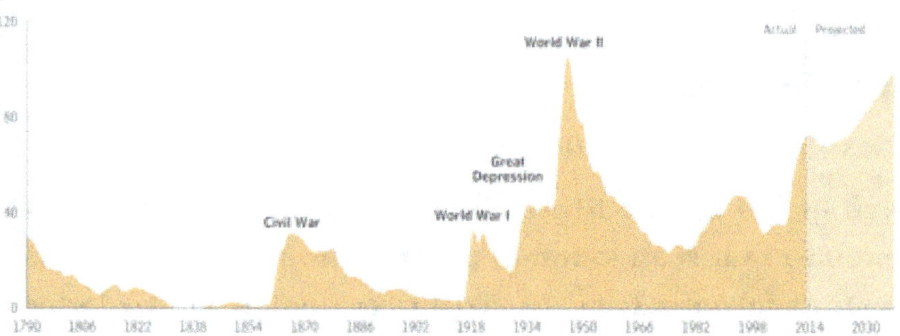

US federal debt held by the public as a percentage of GDP, from 1790 to 2013

[National debt of the United States](#)

The total [national debt](#) in the United States was $18.527 trillion (106% of the GDP), according to an estimate for 2014 by the [International Monetary Fund](#). In January 2015, U.S. federal government debt held by the public was approximately $13 trillion, or about 72% of U.S. GDP. Intra-governmental holdings stood at $5 trillion, giving a combined total debt of $18.080 trillion. By 2012, total federal debt had surpassed 100% of U.S. GDP. The U.S. has a [credit rating](#) of AA+ from [Standard & Poor's](#), AAA from [Fitch](#), and Aaa from[Moody's](#). Historically, the U.S. public debt as a share of GDP increased during wars and recessions, and subsequently declined. For example, debt held by the public as a share of GDP peaked just after World War II (113% of GDP in 1945), but then fell over the following 30 years. In recent decades, large budget deficits and the resulting increases in debt have led to concern about the long-term sustainability of the federal government's fiscal policies. However, these concerns are not universally shared.

Military

[United States Armed Forces](#)

The [carrier strike groups](#) of the *Kitty Hawk*, *Ronald Reagan*, and *Abraham Lincoln* with aircraft from the [Marine Corps](#), [Navy](#), and [Air Force](#).

[Davis-Monthan Air Force Base](#), Tucson, Arizona (February 4, 2004)

The President holds the title of [commander-in-chief](#) of the nation's armed forces and appoints its leaders, the [Secretary of Defense](#) and the [Joint Chiefs of Staff](#). The [United States Department of Defense](#) administers the armed forces, including the [Army](#), [Navy](#), [Marine Corps](#), and [Air Force](#). The [Coast Guard](#) is run by the [Department of Homeland Security](#) in peacetime and by the [Department of the Navy](#) during times of war. In 2008, the armed forces had 1.4 million personnel on active duty. The [Reserves](#) and [National Guard](#) brought the total number of troops to 2.3 million. The Department of Defense also employed about 700,000 civilians, not including contractors.

Military service is voluntary, though [conscription](#) may occur in wartime through the [Selective Service System](#). American forces can be rapidly deployed by the Air Force's large fleet of transport aircraft, the Navy's 10 active aircraft carriers, and [Marine expeditionary units](#) at sea with the Navy's [Atlantic](#) and [Pacific fleets](#). The military operates 865 bases and facilities abroad, and maintains [deployments greater than 100 active duty personnel](#) in 25 foreign countries.

The [military budget of the United States](#) in 2011 was more than $700 billion, 41% of global military spending and equal to the next 14 largest national military expenditures combined. At 4.7% of GDP, the rate was the second-highest among the top 15 military spenders, after [Saudi Arabia](#). U.S. defense spending as a percentage of GDP ranked 23rd globally in 2012 according to the CIA. Defense's share of U.S. spending has generally declined in recent decades, from Cold War peaks of 14.2% of GDP in 1953 and 69.5% of federal outlays in 1954 to 4.7% of GDP and 18.8% of federal outlays in 2011.

The proposed base [Department of Defense budget](#) for 2012, $553 billion, was a 4.2% increase over 2011; an additional $118 billion was proposed for the military campaigns in Iraq and Afghanistan. The last American troops serving in Iraq departed in December 2011;4,484 service members were killed during the [Iraq War](). Approximately 90,000 U.S. troops were serving in Afghanistan in April 2012; by November 8, 2013 2,285 had been killed during the [War in Afghanistan]().

Law enforcement and crime

[Law enforcement in the United States]() and *[Crime in the United States]()*

[Law of the United States](), [Capital punishment in the United States](), [Second Amendment to the United States Constitution]() and *[Human rights in the United States § Justice system]()*

Law enforcement in the U.S. is maintained primarily by local police departments. The [New York City Police Department]() (NYPD) is the largest in the country.

Law enforcement in the United States is primarily the responsibility of local police and [sheriff]()'s departments, with [state police]() providing broader services. Federal agencies such as the [Federal Bureau of Investigation]() (FBI) and the [U.S. Marshals Service]() have specialized duties, including protecting [civil rights](), [national security]() and enforcing [U.S. federal courts]()' rulings and federal laws. At the federal level and in almost every state, a legal system operates on a [common law](). State courts conduct most criminal trials; [federal courts]() handle certain designated crimes as well as certain appeals from the state criminal courts. [Plea bargaining in the United States]() is very common; the vast majority of criminal cases in the country are settled by [plea bargain]() rather than [jury trial]().

In 2012 there were 4.7 murders per 100,000 persons in the United States, a 54% decline from the modern peak of 10.2 in 1980. Among developed nations, the United States has above-average levels of violent crime and particularly high levels of [gun violence]().A cross-sectional analysis of the [World Health Organization]() Mortality Database from 2003 showed that United States "homicide rates were 6.9 times higher than rates in the other high-income countries, driven by firearm homicide rates that were 19.5 times higher." [Gun ownership rights]() continue to be the subject of [contentious political debate](). The

FBI's Uniform Crime Reports estimates that there were 3,246 violent and property crimes per 100,000 residents in 2012, for a total of over 9 million total crimes.

Capital punishment is sanctioned in the United States for certain federal and military crimes, and used in 32 states. No executions took place from 1967 to 1977, owing in part to aU.S. Supreme Court ruling striking down arbitrary imposition of the death penalty. In 1976, that Court ruled that, under appropriate circumstances, capital punishment may constitutionally be imposed. Since the decision there have been more than 1,300 executions, a majority of these taking place in three states: Texas, Virginia, and Oklahoma. Meanwhile, several states have either abolished or struck down death penalty laws. In 2010, the country had the fifth highest number of executions in the world, following China, Iran, North Korea, and Yemen.

The United States has the highest documented incarceration rate and total prison population in the world. At the start of 2008, more than 2.3 million people were incarcerated, more than one in every 100 adults. At year end 2012, the combined U.S. adult correctional systems supervised about 6,937,600 offenders. About 1 in every 35 adult residents in the United States was under some form of correctional supervision at yearend 2012, the lowest rate observed since 1997. The prison population has quadrupled since 1980. However, the imprisonment rate for all prisoners sentenced to more than a year in state or federal facilities is 478 per 100,000 in 2013 and the rate for pre-trial/remand prisoners is 153 per 100,000 residents in 2012. African-American males are jailed at about six times the rate of white males and three times the rate of Hispanic males. The country's high rate of incarceration is largely due to changes in sentencing guidelines and drug policies. According to the Federal Bureau of Prisons, the majority of inmates held in federal prisons are convicted of drug offenses. The privatization of prisons and prison services which began in the 1980s has been the subject of criticism. In 2008, Louisiana had the highest incarceration rate, and Maine the lowest. In 2012, Louisiana had the highest rate of murder and non-negligent manslaughter in the U.S., and New Hampshire the lowest.

Economy

Economy of the United States

Economic indicators

Nominal GDP	$17.555 trillion (Q3 2014)
Real GDP growth	5% (Q3 2014, annualized)
	2.2% (2013)
CPI inflation	2.1% (May 2014)
Employment-to-population ratio	58.9% (May 2014)
Unemployment	5.5% (February 2015)
Labor force participation rate	62.8% (October 2014)
Total public debt	$17.5 trillion (Q2 2014)
Household net worth	$81.8 trillion (Q1 2014)

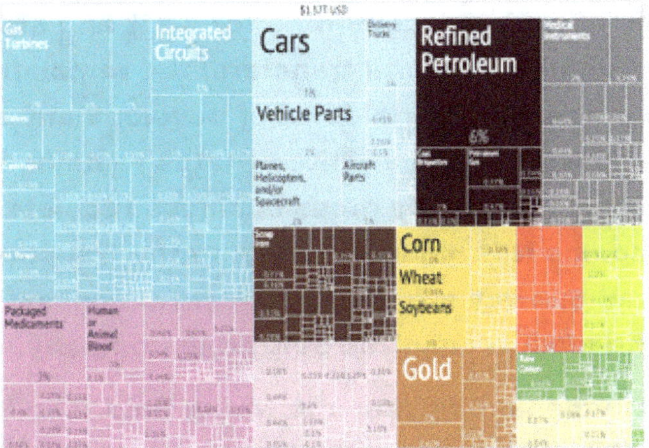

United States export treemap (2011): The U.S. is the world's second-largest exporter.

The United States has a capitalist mixed economy which is fueled by abundant natural resources and high productivity.According to the International Monetary Fund, the U.S. GDP of $16.8 trillion constitutes 24% of the gross world product at market exchange rates and over 19% of the gross world product at purchasing power parity (PPP). Its national GDP was about 5% larger at PPP in 2014 than the European Union's, whose population is around 62% higher. However, the US's nominal GDP is estimated to be $17.528 trillion as of 2014, which is about 5% smaller than that of the European Union. From 1983 to 2008, U.S. real compounded annual GDP growth was 3.3%, compared to a 2.3% weighted average for the rest of the G7. The country ranks ninth in the world in nominal GDP per capita and sixth in GDP per capita at PPP. The U.S. dollar is the world's primary reserve currency.

The United States is the largest importer of goods and second largest exporter, though exports per capita are relatively low. In 2010, the total U.S. trade deficit was $635 billion. Canada, China, Mexico, Japan, and Germany are its top trading partners. In 2010, oil was the largest import commodity, while transportation equipment was the country's largest export. China is the largest foreign holder of U.S. public debt The largest holder of the U.S. debt are American entities, including federal government accounts and the Federal Reserve, who hold the majority of the debt.

The Stockholm International Peace Research Institute, SIPRI, found that the United States' arms industry was the world's biggest exporter of major weapons from 2005-2009, and remained the largest exporter of major weapons during a period between 2010-2014, followed by Russia, China (PRC), and Germany.

In 2009, the private sector was estimated to constitute 86.4% of the economy, with federal government activity accounting for 4.3% and state and local government activity (including federal transfers) the remaining 9.3%. While its economy has reached a postindustrial level of development and its service sector constitutes 67.8% of GDP, the United States remains an industrial power. The leading business field by gross business receipts is wholesale and retail trade; by net income it is manufacturing. In the franchising business model, McDonald's and Subway are the two most recognized brands in the world.Coca-Cola is the most recognized soft drink company in the world.

Chemical products are the leading manufacturing field. The United States is the largest producer of oil in the world, as well as its second largest importer. It is the world's number one producer of electrical and nuclear energy, as well as liquid natural gas, sulfur, phosphates, and salt. The National Mining Association provides data pertaining to coal and minerals that includeberyllium, copper, lead, magnesium, zinc, titanium and others.

Agriculture accounts for just under 1% of GDP,[373] the United States is the world's top producer of corn and soybeans.The National Agricultural Statistics Service maintains agricultural statistics for products that include peanuts, oats, rye, wheat,rice, cotton, corn, barley, hay, sunflowers, and oilseeds. In addition, the United States Department of Agriculture (USDA) provides livestock statistics regarding beef, poultry, pork, and dairy products. The country is the primary developer and grower of genetically modified food, representing half of the world's biotech crops.

Consumer spending comprises 71% of the U.S. economy in 2013. In August 2010, the American labor force consisted of 154.1 million people. With 21.2 million people, government is the leading field of employment. The largest private employment sector is health care and social assistance, with 16.4 million people. About 12% of workers areunionized, compared to 30% in Western Europe. The World Bank ranks the United States first in the ease of hiring and firing workers. The United States is ranked among the top three in the Global Competitiveness Report as well. The United States is the only advanced economy that does not guarantee its workers paid vacation and is one of just a few countries in the world without paid family leave as a legal right, with the others being Papua New Guinea, Suriname and Liberia. However, 74% of full-time American workers get paid sick leave, according to the Bureau of Labor Statistics, although only 24% of part-time workers get the same benefits. While federal law currently does not require sick leave, it's a common benefit for government workers and full-time employees at corporations. In 2009, the United States had the third highest [workforce productivity](#) per person in the world, behind [Luxembourg](#) and [Norway](#). It was fourth in productivity per hour, behind those two countries and the [Netherlands](#).

The [2008-2012 global recession](#) had a significant impact on the United States, with output still below potential according to the [Congressional Budget Office](#). It brought high[unemployment](#) (which has been decreasing but remains above pre-recession levels), along with low [consumer confidence](#), the [continuing decline in home values and increase in foreclosures and personal bankruptcies](#), an escalating federal debt crisis, [inflation](#), and [rising petroleum and food prices](#). There remains a record proportion of [long-term unemployed](#), continued decreasing [household income](#), and tax and [federal budget increases](#). A 2011 poll found that more than half of all Americans think the U.S. is still in recession or even [depression](#), despite official data that shows a historically modest recovery. In 2013 the [Census Bureau](#) defined poverty rate decreased to roughly 14.5% of the population.

Income, poverty and wealth

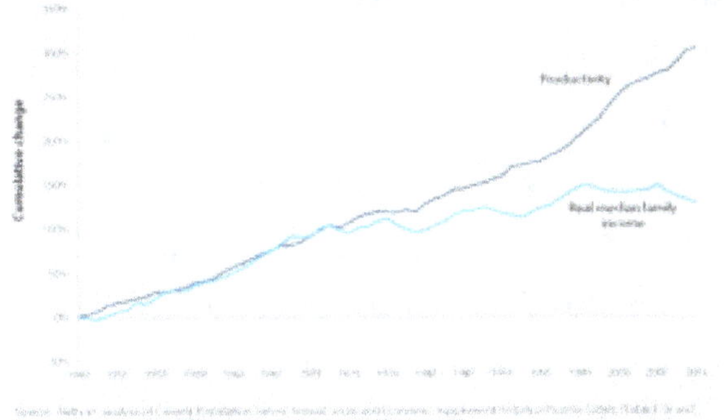

A [tract housing](#) development in [San Jose, California](#)

Further information: [Income in the United States](#), [Poverty in the United States](#), [Affluence in the United States](#), [United States counties by per capita income](#) and [Income inequality in the United States](#)

Americans have the highest average household and employee income among OECD nations, and in 2007 had the second highest median household income. According to the Census Bureau real median household income was $50,502 in 2011, down from $51,144 in 2010. The Global Food Security Index ranked the U.S. number one for food affordability and overall food security in March 2013.Americans on average have over twice as much living space per dwelling and per person as European Union residents, and more than every EU nation. For 2013 the United Nations Development Programme ranked the United States 5th among 187 countries in itsHuman Development Index and 28th in its inequality-adjusted HDI (IHDI).

There has been a widening gap between productivity and median incomes since the 1970s. While inflation-adjusted ("real") household income had been increasing almost every year from 1947 to 1999, it has since been flat and even decreased recently. The rise in the share of total annual income received by the top 1 percent, which has more than doubled from 9 percent in 1976 to 20 percent in 2011, has had a significant impact on income inequality, leaving the United States with one of the widest income distributions among OECD nations.The post-recession income gains have been very uneven, with the top 1 percent capturing 95 percent of the income gains from 2009 to 2012.

Wealth, like income and taxes, is highly concentrated; the richest 10% of the adult population possess 72% of the country's household wealth, while the bottom half claim only 2%. Between June 2007 and November 2008 the global recession led to falling asset prices around the world. Assets owned by Americans lost about a quarter of their value. Since peaking in the second quarter of 2007, household wealth is down $14 trillion.At the end of 2008, household debt amounted to $13.8 trillion.

There were about 643,000 sheltered and unsheltered homeless persons in the U.S. in January 2009, with almost two-thirds staying in an emergency shelter or transitional housing program. In 2011 16.7 million children lived in food-insecure households, about 35% more than 2007 levels, though only 1.1% of U.S. children, or 845,000, saw reduced food intake or disrupted eating patterns at some point during the year, and most cases were not chronic. According to a 2014 report by the Census Bureau, one in five young adults lives inpoverty today, up from one in seven in 1980.

Education

Education in the United States

The University of Virginia, founded by Thomas Jefferson in 1819, is one of the many public universities in the United States.

American public education is operated by state and local governments, regulated by the United States Department of Education through restrictions on federal grants. In most states, children are required to attend school from the age of six or seven (generally, kindergarten or first grade) until they turn 18 (generally bringing them through twelfth grade, the end of high school); some states allow students to leave school at 16 or 17. About 12% of children are enrolled in parochial or nonsectarian private schools. Just over 2% of children are homeschooled.The U.S. spends more on education per student than any nation in the world, spending more than $11,000 per elementary student in 2010 and more than $12,000 per high school student. Some 80% of U.S. college students attend public universities.

The United States has many competitive private and public institutions of higher education. According to prominent international rankings, 13 or 15 American colleges and universities are ranked among the top 20 in the world. There are also local community colleges with generally more open admission policies, shorter academic programs, and lower tuition. Of Americans 25 and older, 84.6% graduated from high school, 52.6% attended some college, 27.2% earned a bachelor's degree, and 9.6% earned graduate degrees. The basic literacy rate is approximately 99%. The United Nations assigns the United States an Education Index of 0.97, tying it for 12th in the world.

As for public expenditures on higher education, the U.S. trails some other OECD nations but spends more per student than the OECD average, and more than all nations in combined public and private spending. As of 2012, student loan debt exceeded one trillion dollars, more than Americans owe on credit cards.

Culture

Culture of the United States

Alaska Natives § Cultures, *Native American cultures in the United States*, *Culture of the Native Hawaiians*, *Social class in the United States*, *Public holidays in the United States* and *Tourism in the United States*

The United States is home to many cultures and a wide variety of ethnic groups, traditions, and values. Aside from the Native American, Native Hawaiian and Native Alaskanpopulations, nearly all Americans or their ancestors settled or immigrated within the past five centuries. Mainstream American culture is a Western culture largely derived from thetraditions of European immigrants with influences from many other sources, such as traditions brought by slaves from Africa. More recent immigration from Asia and especiallyLatin America has added to a cultural mix that has been described as both a homogenizing melting pot, and a heterogeneous salad bowl in which immigrants and their descendants retain distinctive cultural characteristics.

Core American culture was established by Protestant British colonists and shaped by the frontier settlement process, with the traits derived passed down to descendants and transmitted to immigrants through assimilation. Americans have traditionally been characterized by a strong work ethic, competitiveness, and individualism, as well as a unifying belief in an "American creed" emphasizing liberty, equality, private property, democracy, rule of law, and a preference for limited government. Americans are extremely charitable by global standards. According to a 2006 British study, Americans gave 1.67% of GDP to charity, more than any other nation studied, more than twice the second place British figure of 0.73%, and around twelve times the French figure of 0.14%.The American Dream, or the perception that Americans enjoy high social mobility, plays a key role in attracting immigrants. Whether this perception is realistic has been a topic of debate. While mainstream culture holds that the United States is a classless society, scholars identify significant differences between the country's social classes, affecting socialization, language, and values. Americans' self-images, social viewpoints, and cultural expectations are associated with their occupations to an unusually close degree. While Americans tend greatly to value socioeconomic achievement, being ordinary or average is generally seen as a positive attribute.

Food

Cuisine of the United States

[Apple pie](#) is a food commonly associated with American cuisine.

Mainstream American cuisine is similar to that in other Western countries. [Wheat](#) is the primary cereal grain with about three-quarters of grain products made of wheat flour and many dishes use indigenous ingredients, such as turkey, venison, potatoes, sweet potatoes, corn, squash, and maple syrup which were consumed by [Native Americans](#) and early European settlers.These home grown foods are part of a shared national menu on one of America's most popular holidays; [Thanksgiving](#), when some Americans make traditional foods to celebrate the occasion.

Roasted turkey is a traditional menu item of an American [Thanksgiving](#) dinner.

Characteristic dishes such as apple pie, fried chicken, pizza, hamburgers, and hot dogs derive from the recipes of various immigrants. French fries, Mexican dishes such as burritos and tacos, and pasta dishes freely adapted from [Italian](#) sources are widely consumed. Americans generally prefer coffee to tea. Marketing by U.S. industries is largely responsible for making orange juice and milk ubiquitous [breakfast](#) beverages.

American eating habits owe a great deal to that of their [British culinary](#) roots with some variations. Even though American lands could grow newer vegetables England could not, most colonist would not eat these new foods until accepted by Europeans. Over time American foods changed to a point that food critic, [John L. Hess](#) stated in 1972: *"Our founding fathers were as far superior to our present political leaders in the quality of their food as they were in the quality of their prose and intelligence"*.

The American fast food industry, the world's largest, pioneered the drive-through format in the 1940s. Fast food consumption has sparked health concerns. During the 1980s and 1990s, Americans' caloric intake rose 24%; frequent dining at fast food outlets is associated with what public health officials call the American "obesity epidemic". Highly sweetened soft drinks are widely popular, and sugared beverages account for nine percent of American caloric intake.

Literature, philosophy, and the arts

American literature, American philosophy, Visual art of the United States and American classical music

In the 18th and early 19th centuries, American art and literature took most of its cues from Europe. Writers such as Nathaniel Hawthorne, Edgar Allan Poe, and Henry David Thoreau established a distinctive American literary voice by the middle of the 19th century. Mark Twain and poet Walt Whitman were major figures in the century's second half; Emily Dickinson, virtually unknown during her lifetime, is now recognized as an essential American poet. A work seen as capturing fundamental aspects of the national experience and character—such as Herman Melville's *Moby-Dick* (1851), Twain's *The Adventures of Huckleberry Finn* (1885), and F. Scott Fitzgerald's *The Great Gatsby* (1925)—may be dubbed the "Great American Novel".

Mark Twain, American author and humorist

Eleven U.S. citizens have won the Nobel Prize in Literature, most recently Toni Morrison in 1993. William Faulkner and Ernest Hemingway are often named among the most influential writers of the 20th century. Popular literary genres such as the Western and hardboiled crime fiction developed in the United States. The Beat Generation writers opened up new literary approaches, as have postmodernist authors such as John Barth, Thomas Pynchon, and Don DeLillo.

The transcendentalists, led by Thoreau and Ralph Waldo Emerson, established the first major American philosophical movement. After the Civil War,Charles Sanders Peirce and then William James and John Dewey were leaders in the development of pragmatism. In the 20th century, the work of W. V. O. Quine and Richard Rorty, and later Noam Chomsky, brought analytic philosophy to the fore of American philosophical academia. John Rawls andRobert Nozick led a revival of political philosophy. Cornel West and Judith Butler have led a continental tradition in American philosophical academia. Globally influential Chicago school economists like Milton Friedman, James M. Buchanan, and Thomas Sowell have transcended discipline to impact various fields in social and political philosophy.

In the visual arts, the Hudson River School was a mid-19th-century movement in the tradition of European naturalism. The realist paintings of Thomas Eakins are now widely celebrated. The 1913 Armory Show in New York City, an exhibition of European modernist art, shocked the public and transformed the U.S. art scene.Georgia O'Keeffe, Marsden Hartley, and others experimented with new, individualistic styles. Major artistic movements such as the abstract expressionism of Jackson Pollock and Willem de Kooning and the pop art of Andy Warhol and Roy Lichtensteindeveloped largely in the United States. The tide of modernism and then postmodernism has brought fame to American architects such as Frank Lloyd Wright, Philip Johnson, and Frank Gehry.

Times Square in New York City, the hub of the Broadway theater district

One of the first major promoters of [American theater](#) was impresario [P. T. Barnum](#), who began operating a lower [Manhattan](#) entertainment complex in 1841. The team of [Harrigan and Hart](#) produced a series of popular [musical](#) comedies in New York starting in the late 1870s. In the 20th century, the modern musical form emerged on [Broadway](#); the songs of musical theater composers such as [Irving Berlin](#), [Cole Porter](#), and [Stephen Sondheim](#) have become [pop standards](#). Playwright [Eugene O'Neill](#) won the Nobel literature prize in 1936; other acclaimed U.S. dramatists include multiple [Pulitzer Prize](#) winners [Tennessee Williams](#), [Edward Albee](#), and [August Wilson](#).

Though little known at the time, [Charles Ives](#)'s work of the 1910s established him as the first major U.S. composer in the classical tradition, while experimentalists such as [Henry Cowell](#) and [John Cage](#) created a distinctive American approach to classical composition. [Aaron Copland](#)and [George Gershwin](#) developed a new synthesis of popular and classical music. [Choreographers](#) [Isadora Duncan](#) and [Martha Graham](#) helped create [modern dance](#), while [George Balanchine](#) and [Jerome Robbins](#) were leaders in 20th-century ballet. Americans have long been important in the modern artistic medium of [photography](#), with major photographers including [Alfred Stieglitz](#), [Edward Steichen](#), and [Ansel Adams](#).[466]

Music
Music of the United States

[Elvis Presley](#)

The rhythmic and lyrical styles of [African-American music](#) have deeply influenced [American music](#) at large, distinguishing it from European traditions. Elements from [folk](#) idioms such as the [blues](#) and what is now known as [old-time music](#) were adopted and transformed into [popular genres](#) with global audiences. [Jazz](#) was developed by innovators such as [Louis Armstrong](#) and [Duke Ellington](#) early in the 20th century. [Country music](#) developed in the 1920s, and [rhythm and blues](#) in the 1940s.

[Elvis Presley](#) and [Chuck Berry](#) were among the mid-1950s pioneers of [rock and roll](#). In the 1960s, [Bob Dylan](#) emerged from the [folk revival](#) to become one of America's most celebrated songwriters and [James Brown](#) led the development of [funk](#). More recent American creations include [hip hop](#) and[house music](#). American pop stars such as Presley, [Michael Jackson](#), and [Madonna](#) have become global celebrities, as have contemporary musical artists such as [Lady Gaga](#), [Taylor Swift](#), [Katy Perry](#), [Rihanna](#), and [Beyoncé](#).

Cinema

[Cinema of the United States](#)

The [Hollywood Sign](#) in [Los Angeles, California](#)

[Hollywood](#), a northern district of [Los Angeles](#), California, is one of the leaders in motion picture production. The world's first commercial motion picture exhibition was given in New York City in 1894, using [Thomas Edison](#)'s [Kinetoscope](#). The next year saw the first commercial screening of a projected film, also in New York, and the United States was in the forefront of [sound film](#)'s development in the following decades. Since the early 20th century, the U.S. film industry has largely been based in and around Hollywood, although in the 21st century an increasing number of films are not made there, and film companies have been subject to the forces of globalization.

[Marilyn Monroe](), an icon of Hollywood

Director [D. W. Griffith](), American's top filmmaker during the silent film period, was central to the development of [film grammar](), and producer/entrepreneur [Walt Disney]() was a leader in both [animated film]() and movie [merchandising](). Directors such as [John Ford]() redefined the image of the American Old West and history, and, like others such as [John Huston](), broadened the possibilities of cinema with location shooting, with great influence on subsequent directors. The industry enjoyed its golden years, in what is commonly referred to as the "[Golden Age of Hollywood]()", from the early sound period until the early 1960s, with screen actors such as [John Wayne]() and [Marilyn Monroe]() becoming iconic figures. In the 1970s, film directors such as [Martin Scorsese](), [Francis Ford Coppola]() and [Robert Altman]() were a vital component in what became known as "[New Hollywood]()" or the "Hollywood Renaissance", grittier films influenced by French and Italian realist pictures of the post-war period. Since, directors such as [Steven Spielberg](), [George Lucas]() and [James Cameron]() have gained renown for their blockbuster films, often characterized by high production costs, and in return, high earnings at the box office, with Cameron's *Avatar* (2009) earning more than $2 billion. Notable films topping the [American Film Institute]()'s [AFI 100]() list include [Orson Welles]()'s *Citizen Kane* (1941), which is frequently cited as the greatest film of all time, *Casablanca* (1942), *The Godfather* (1972), *Gone with the Wind* (1939), *Lawrence of Arabia* (1962), *The Wizard of Oz* (1939), *The Graduate* (1967), *On the Waterfront* (1954), *Schindler's List* (1993), *Singin' in the Rain* (1952), *It's a Wonderful Life* (1946) and *Sunset Boulevard* (1950). The [Academy Awards](), popularly known as the Oscars, have been held annually by the [Academy of Motion Picture Arts and Sciences]() since 1929, and the [Golden Globe Awards]() have been held annually since January 1944.

Sports

Sports in the United States

Swimmer [Michael Phelps](#)and then-President [George W. Bush](#) August 10, 2008 at the National Aquatic Center in[Beijing](#). Phelps is the most decorated [Olympic athlete](#) of all time.

While most major U.S. sports have evolved out of European practices, [basketball](#), [volleyball](#), [skateboarding](#), and [snowboarding](#) are American inventions, some of which have become popular in other countries. [Lacrosse](#) and [surfing](#) arose from Native American and Native Hawaiian activities that predate Western contact.[482] The [Iroquois](#) field their own separate national team, the [Iroquois Nationals](#), in recognition of the confederacy's creation of lacrosse. Eight [Olympic Games](#) have [taken place in the United States.](#) The United States has won 2,400 medals at the [Summer Olympic Games](#), more than any other country, and 281 in the [Winter Olympic Games](#), the second most behind [Norway](#).

The market for professional sports in the United States is roughly $69 billion, roughly 50% larger than that of all of Europe, the Middle East, and Africa combined. [Baseball](#) has been regarded as the [national sport](#) since the late 19th century, with [Major League Baseball](#) (MLB) being the top league, while [American football](#) is now by several measures the most popular spectator sport, with the [National Football League](#) (NFL) having the highest average attendance of any sports league in the world and a [Super Bowl](#) watched by millions globally. [Basketball](#) and [ice hockey](#) are the country's next two leading professional team sports, with the top leagues being the [National Basketball Association](#) (NBA) and the [National Hockey League](#) (NHL). These four major sports, when played professionally, each occupy a season at different, but overlapping, times of the year. [College football](#) and[basketball](#) attract large audiences. [Boxing](#) and [horse racing](#) were once the most watched [individual sports](#), but they have been eclipsed by [golf](#)and [auto racing](#), particularly NASCAR. In the 21st century, televised mixed martial arts has also gained a strong following of regular viewers.While soccer is less popular in the United States than in many other nations, the country hosted the 1994 FIFA World Cup, the men's national soccer team has been to the past six World Cups and the women are first in the women's world rankings.

Infrastructure

Transportation

Transportation in the United States

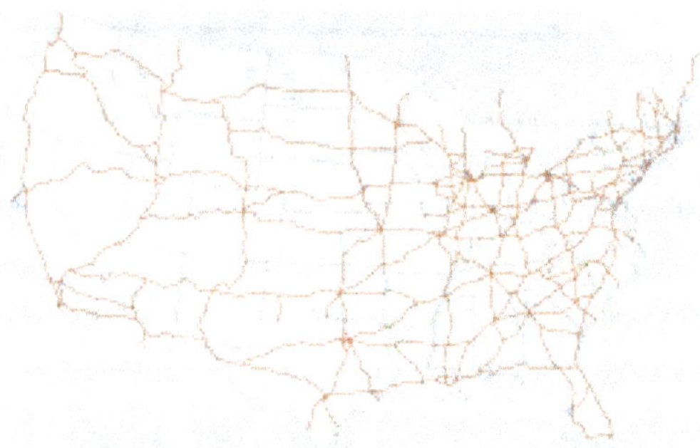

The Interstate Highway System, which extends 46,876 miles (75,440 km)

Personal transportation is dominated by automobiles, which operate on a network of 4 million miles of public roads, including one of the world's longest highway systems.The world's second largest automobile market, the United States has the highest rate of per-capita vehicle ownership in the world, with 765 vehicles per 1,000 Americans. About 40% of personal vehicles are vans, SUVs, or light trucks. The average American adult (accounting for all drivers and non-drivers) spends 55 minutes driving every day, traveling 29 miles (47 km).

Mass transit accounts for 9% of total U.S. work trips. While transport of goods by rail is extensive, relatively few people use rail to travel, though ridership on Amtrak, the national intercity passenger rail system, grew by almost 37% between 2000 and 2010. Also,light rail development has increased in recent years. Bicycle usage for work commutes is minimal.

The civil airline industry is entirely privately owned and has been largely deregulated since 1978, while most major airports are publicly owned. The three largest airlines in the world by passengers carried are U.S.-based; American Airlines is number one after its 2013 acquisition by US Airways. Of the world's 30 busiest passenger airports, 12 are in the United States, including the busiest, Hartsfield–Jackson Atlanta International Airport.

Energy

The [Hoover Dam](#) when completed in 1936 was both the world's largest electric-power generating station and the world's largest [concrete](#) structure.

Energy policy of the United States

The [United States energy](#) market is about 29,000 [terawatt hours](#) per year. [Energy consumption per capita](#) is 7.8 tons of oil equivalent per year, the 10th highest rate in the world. In 2005, 40% of this energy came from petroleum, 23% from coal, and 22% from natural gas. The remainder was supplied by nuclear power and [renewable energy](#) sources. The United States is the world's largest consumer of petroleum.

For decades, [nuclear power](#) has played a limited role relative to many other developed countries, in part because of public perception in the wake of a [1979 accident](#). In 2007, several applications for new nuclear plants were filed. The United States has 27% of global coal reserves. It is the world's largest producer of natural gas and crude oil.

Science and technology

Science and technology in the United States

Technological and industrial history of the United States

Astronaut [James Irwin](#) walking on the [Moon](#) next to [Apollo 15](#)'s [landing module](#) and [lunar rover](#) in 1971. The effort to reach the Moon was triggered by the [Space Race](#).

The United States has been a leader in scientific research and technological innovation since the late 19th century. In 1876, Alexander Graham Bell was awarded the first U.S. patent for the telephone. Thomas Edison's research laboratory, one of the first of its kind, developed the phonograph, the first long-lasting light bulb, and the first viable movie camera. The latter lead to emergence of the worldwide entertainment industry. In the early 20th century, the automobile companies of Ransom E. Olds and Henry Ford popularized the assembly line. The Wright brothers, in 1903, made the first sustained and controlled heavier-than-air powered flight.

The rise of Nazism in the 1930s led many European scientists, including Albert Einstein, Enrico Fermi, and John von Neumann, to immigrate to the United States. During World War II, the Manhattan Project developed nuclear weapons, ushering in the Atomic Age, while the Space Race produced rapid advances in rocketry, materials science, and aeronautics.

The invention of the transistor in the 1950s, a key active component in practically all modern electronics, lead to many technological developments and a significant expansion of the U.S. technology industry. This in turn lead to the establishment of many new technology companies and regions around the county such as Silicon Valley in California. Advancements by American microprocessor companies such as Advanced Micro Devices (AMD), and Intel along with both computer software and hardware companies that include Adobe Systems, Apple Computer, IBM, GNU-Linux, Microsoft, and Sun Microsystems created and popularized the personal computer. The ARPANET was developed in the 1960s to meet Defense Department requirements, and became the first of a series of networks which evolved into the Internet.

These advancements then lead to greater personalization of technology for individual use. As of April 2010, 77% of American households owned at least one computer, and 68% had broadband Internet service. 85% of Americans also own a mobile phone as of 2011. The United States ranks highly with regard to freedom of use of the internet.

In the 21st century, 64% of research and development funding comes from the private sector. The United States leads the world in scientific research papers and impact factor.

Health

Health care in the United States, *Health care reform in the United States* and *Health insurance in the United States*

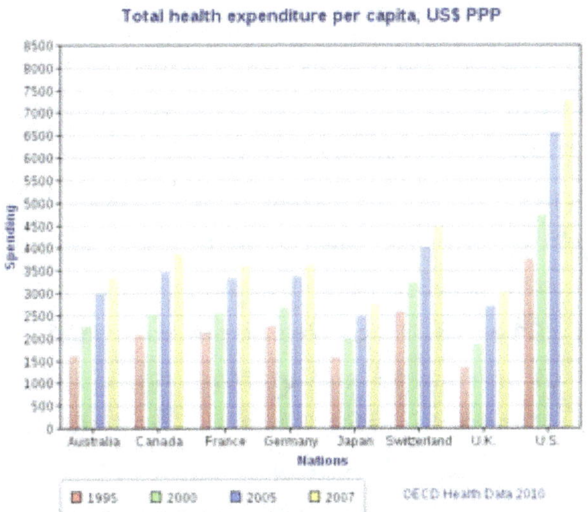

Health spending per capita, in US$ PPP-adjusted, compared amongst various first world nations.

The United States has a life expectancy of 79.8 years at birth, up from 75.2 years in 1990.Increasing obesity in the United States and health improvements elsewhere have contributed to lowering the country's rank in life expectancy from 1987, when it was 11th in the world. Obesity rates in the United States are among the highest in the world. Approximately one-third of the adult population is obese and an additional third is overweight; the obesity rate, the highest in the industrialized world, has more than doubled in the last quarter-century. Obesity-related type 2 diabetes is considered epidemic by health care professionals. The infant mortality rate of 6.17 per thousand places the United States 169th highest out of 224 countries, with the 224th country having the lowest mortality rate.

In 2010, coronary artery disease, lung cancer, stroke, chronic obstructive pulmonary diseases, and traffic accidents caused the most years of life lost in the U.S. Low back pain, depression, musculoskeletal disorders, neck pain, and anxiety caused the most years lost to disability. The most deleterious risk factors were poor diet, tobacco smoking, obesity, high blood pressure, high blood sugar, physical inactivity, and alcohol use. Alzheimer's disease, drug abuse, kidney disease and cancer, and falls caused the most additional years of life lost over their age-adjusted 1990 per-capita rates. U.S. teenage pregnancy and abortion rates are substantially higher than in other Western nations, especially among blacks and Hispanics. U.S. underage drinking among teenagers is among the lowest in industrialized nations.

The U.S. is a global leader in medical innovation. America solely developed or contributed significantly to 9 of the top 10 most important medical innovations since 1975 as ranked by a 2001 poll of physicians, while the EU and Switzerland together contributed to five. Since 1966, more Americans have received the [Nobel Prize in Medicine](#) than the rest of the world combined. From 1989 to 2002, four times more money was invested in private biotechnology companies in America than in Europe. The U.S. health-care system far [outspends](#) any other nation, measured in both per capita spending and percentage of GDP. Health-care coverage in the United States is a combination of public and private efforts and is not [universal](#). In 2014, 13.4% of the population did not carry [health insurance](#). The subject of uninsured and underinsured Americans is a major political issue. In 2006, [Massachusetts](#) became the first state to mandate universal health insurance. [Federal legislation](#) passed in early 2010 would ostensibly create a near-universal health insurance system around the country by 2014, though the bill and its ultimate impact are issues of controversy.

Media

[Media of the United States](#) and [Television in the United States](#)

Corporate headquarters of the [American Broadcasting Company](#) in New York City

The four major broadcasters in the U.S. are the [National Broadcasting Company](#) (NBC), [Columbia Broadcasting System](#) (CBS), the [American Broadcasting Company](#) (ABC) and [Fox](#). Americans are the heaviest television viewers in the world,and the average viewing time continues to rise, reaching five hours a day in 2006. The four major broadcast [television networks](#) are all commercial entities. Americans listen to radio programming, also largely commercial, on average just over two-and-a-half hours a day.

In 1998, the number of U.S. commercial radio stations had grown to 4,793 AM stations and 5,662 FM stations. In addition, there are 1,460 public radio stations. Most of these stations are run by universities and public authorities for educational purposes and are financed by public or private funds, subscriptions and corporate underwriting. Much public-radio broadcasting is supplied by NPR (formerly National Public Radio). NPR was incorporated in February 1970 under the Public Broadcasting Act of 1967; its television counterpart, PBS, was also created by the same legislation. (NPR and PBS are operated separately from each other.) As of September 30, 2014 there are 15,433 licensed full-power radio stations in the US according to the FCC.

Well-known newspapers are *The New York Times*, *USA Today* and *The Wall Street Journal*. Although the cost of publishing has increased over the years, the price of newspapers has generally remained low, forcing newspapers to rely more on advertising revenue and on articles provided by a major wire service, such as the Associated Press or Reuters, for their national and world coverage. With very few exceptions, all the newspapers in the U.S. are privately owned, either by large chains such as Gannett or McClatchy, which own dozens or even hundreds of newspapers; by small chains that own a handful of papers; or in a situation that is increasingly rare, by individuals or families. Major cities often have "alternative weeklies" to complement the mainstream daily paper(s), for example, New York City's *The Village Voice* or Los Angeles' *LA Weekly*, to name two of the best-known. Major cities may also support a local business journal, trade papers relating to local industries, and papers for local ethnic and social groups. Early versions of the American newspaper comic strip and the American comic book began appearing in the 19th century. In 1938, Superman, the quintessential comic book superhero of DC Comics, developed into an American icon. Aside from web portals and search engines, the most popular websites are Facebook, YouTube, Wikipedia, Amazon, eBay, and Twitter.

In Spanish, the second most widely spoken mother tongue behind English, more than 800 publications are published.

Facts that shows that America is no longer the land of the free and home to the brave:

Now the truth of the matter, with the recent happenings in the United States, one will be forced to ask if the United States is still the land of the free and home to the brave. A free land is a place where humans finds comfort knowing full well that their lives and properties are safe and that nobody is going to hate then because of their color and nationality.

United States of America was once a peaceful and loving country to be in, a place where lives and properties are valued and taking care of. But the United State today is the opposite of the United States yesterday, cowards have taken over the peace and unity the states once enjoyed, racism, rampard death, hate and police brutality are now the order of the day. The blacks in the United States lives in total fear putting in mind that they can die at any time in the hands of racist police, the whites puts hate in their heart saying the blacks have taken over the State. Oh great America, the unity that binds you all is broken, and when you break the hedges, the serpent shall bite. For over two years, I have been doing research and talking to some individual on what they feel about the United State and their answer points to one direction, Racism, Hates and Police brutality. The American government gives right for it citizen to posses fire arms all in the name of protection, that same government turned around to cal the people Thugs, is that been brave? American government are the most terrible cowards the world has ever had, a government who know the truth but refuse to say it, a government who takes delight in the death of it citizen all because of race and nationality. Any country that allows gun in the hands of every one all in the name of protection can never be a free land because the death rate, brutality and lot more will be high. Given guns to everyone is given every one the license to kill at any slight provocation. Gun control is not even the solution, I think gun eradication will do just well. The world now sees the United States as a terror land instead of a free land. The worst crime any one can commit in life is to hate anyone because of its color and that is what is going on in the States.

I meant a friend from the States who came to North Cyprus for his summer holiday last year, and when I asked him what he got to say about the happenings in the States, he gave me a straight answer "problematic government". He went further to say when the government of a land know the truth and just totally refuse to tell the truth, then that land is doomed. The United States have a big problem of race and the government is acting as if all is well. What will you say about a white guy who entered a black church and killed Nine person all because of hate for the black race in America, and instead of the truth to be told, some sick and coward politician are trying to wave the matter and affiliating the attack to religion and mental problem, how coward could that be? A racist guy killing innocent people because he was afraid that blacks are taking over

America. What a shame, what has America become, what happened to the dream Martin Luther King has you oh American? If the government of Australia can overcome racism and gun brutality why can't American overcome? Why is the white police targeting the black community, what gain will you have by eradication the black people from America, what gain do you derive by giving negative sign to the world about you and your government. You hate people simply because of their color and you come out to lie to the world about America been a free land and home to the brave. Let me site some instance why I totally disagree with this phrase "Land of the free and home to the brave".

With police officers escaping prosecution for crimes against the public, and instances of wrongful arrest making headlines, many wonder if America is truly the land of the free. Eric Garner and Michael Brown are but two names of many in the United States (U.S.) that have become synonymous with the justice system failing to protect its citizens. The past several years have seen the rise of so called "criminals" such as the hacker group anonymous taking measures into their own hands. To many, groups such as this act as the legend of Robin Hood did centuries before, though what is being stolen and given to the public is not money but information.

While groups like anonymous do commit felonious acts to get said information, some believe that groups like this would not exist if the system they rebel against actually worked. In a recent study, it was reported that over the past 20 years in America over 2,000 defendants were wrongfully charged and convicted of crimes they did not commit. This is a low estimate. Living in the modern age of information and new DNA evidence coming to light has helped to exonerate a great number of citizens falsely convicted of crimes. Those who have seen the film *The Shawshank Redemption* have some kind of an understanding as to what these cases look like.

Many such cases of wrongful imprisonment come about as a result of persons giving false confessions to police. While the idea of confessing to a crime one did not commit may seem ludicrous, the pressures those under interrogation are put under can make even the strongest willed crack under pressure. Put in positions that include 20 or 30 hour long interrogations without proper representation being present, the stress is enough to goad out a confession to crimes that were never committed. At a time when government agencies are able to access a person's Facebook information to collect data, calling America the land of the free does not seem truthful.

In Ohio, a man named Ricky Jackson was just exonerated after spending 39 years in prison for a murder he did not commit. Wrongfully charged with murder in 1975, Jackson sat in prison wasting away until the only witness to the alleged murder came forward to completely recant their testimony. Jackson spent more time in prison than any other who has been exonerated. While many prosecutors in America are hardly willing to admit their mistakes, those involved in this case seem sincere in their actions. It has been decided that Jackson will receive upwards of a million dollars for the time he spent in prison. Jackson himself stated that he, "really has to take his hat off to the prosecutors and the state for admitting their errors." It would appear that justice is served in America, though it may take 39 years to get there.

Unfortunately, Jackson's case is only one of many that have innocent civilians sitting in jail cells for crimes they never committed. Over 900 days ago in Portland, Oregon, a citizen named Benito Vasquez-Hernandez and his son Moises were placed in custody for allegedly hindering prosecution. Later, the charges which held the two Hernandez men were dropped, yet still they remained in custody. The prosecutor's story now is that the two gentleman are being held in custody as material witnesses in a murder charge being brought against another of their family. Though the prosecutor, Jeff Lesowski, says he "sincerely regrets holding the men in custody", Lesowski claims he has no other choice.

In America, it seems, there is no limit to what a person can be imprisoned for. In cases such as the younger Hernandez, Moises, it has been said by the man's lawyer that the time incarcerated has driven him "literally crazy". While upon his initial arrest there had been no signs of mental illness, Moises has since been diagnosed with schizophrenia, allegedly caused by being incarcerated for committing no crime. What a terrifying concept, to be imprisoned for committing no crimes and going insane as a result.

According to a recent report from the National Registry of Exoneration, over 125 different individuals were exonerated in 2014. With numbers such as those rising every year, critics of the justice system have solid ground to claim that America is not the "land of the free" as some propaganda would lead the world to believe.

Every year, the State Department issues reports on individual rights in other countries, monitoring the passage of restrictive laws and regulations around the world. Iran, for example, has been criticized for denying fair public trials and limiting privacy, while Russia has been taken to task for undermining due process. Other countries have been condemned for the use of secret evidence and torture.

Even as we pass judgment on countries we consider unfree, Americans remain confident that any definition of a free nation must include their own — the land of free. Yet, the laws and practices of the land should shake that confidence. In the decade since Sept. 11, 2001, this country has comprehensively reduced civil liberties in the name of an expanded security state. The most recent example of this was the National Defense Authorization Act, signed Dec. 31, which allows for the indefinite detention of citizens. At what point does the reduction of individual rights in our country change how we define ourselves?

While each new national security power Washington has embraced was controversial when enacted, they are often discussed in isolation. But they don't operate in isolation. They form a mosaic of powers under which our country could be considered, at least in part, authoritarian. Americans often proclaim our nation as a symbol of freedom to the world while dismissing nations such as Cuba and China as categorically unfree. Yet, objectively, we may be only half right. Those countries do lack basic individual rights such as due process, placing them outside any reasonable definition of "free," but the United States now has much more in common with such regimes than anyone may like to admit.

These countries also have constitutions that purport to guarantee freedoms and rights. But their governments have broad discretion in denying those rights and few real avenues for challenges by citizens — precisely the problem with the new laws in this country.

The list of powers acquired by the U.S. government since 9/11 puts us in rather troubling company.

Assassination of U.S. citizens

President Obama has claimed, as President George W. Bush did before him, the right to order the killing of any citizen considered a terrorist or an abettor of terrorism. Last year, he approved the killing of U.S. citizen Anwar al-Awlaqi and another citizen under this claimed inherent authority. Last month, administration officials affirmed that power, stating that the president can order the assassination of any citizen whom he considers allied with terrorists. (Nations such as Nigeria, Iran and Syria have been routinely criticized for extrajudicial killings of enemies of the state.)

Indefinite detention

Under the law signed last month, terrorism suspects are to be held by the military; the president also has the authority to indefinitely detain citizens accused of terrorism. While the administration claims that this provision only codified existing law, experts widely contest this view, and the administration has opposed efforts to challenge such authority in federal courts. The government continues to claim the right to strip citizens of legal protections based on its sole discretion. (China recently codified a more limited detention law for its citizens, while countries such as Cambodia have been singled out by the United States for "prolonged detention.")

Arbitrary justice

The president now decides whether a person will receive a trial in the federal courts or in a military tribunal, a system that has been ridiculed around the world for lacking basic due process protections. Bush claimed this authority in 2001, and Obama has continued the practice. (Egypt and China have been denounced for maintaining separate military justice systems for selected defendants, including civilians.)

Warrantless searches

The president may now order warrantless surveillance, including a new capability to force companies and organizations to turn over information on citizens' finances, communications and associations. Bush acquired this sweeping power under the Patriot Act in 2001, and in 2011, Obama extended the power, including searches of everything from business documents to library records. The government can use "national security letters" to demand, without probable cause, that organizations turn over information on citizens — and order them not to reveal the disclosure to the affected party. (Saudi Arabia and Pakistan operate under laws that allow the government to engage in widespread discretionary surveillance.)

Secret evidence

The government now routinely uses secret evidence to detain individuals and employs secret evidence in federal and military courts. It also forces the dismissal of cases against the United States by simply filing declarations that the cases would make the government reveal classified information that would harm national security — a claim made in a variety of privacy lawsuits and largely accepted by federal judges without question. Even legal opinions, cited as the basis for the government's actions under the Bush and Obama administrations, have been classified. This allows the government to claim secret legal arguments to support secret proceedings using secret evidence. In addition, some cases never make it to court at all. The federal courts routinely deny constitutional challenges to policies and programs under a narrow definition of standing to bring a case.

War crimes

The world clamored for prosecutions of those responsible for waterboarding terrorism suspects during the Bush administration, but the Obama administration said in 2009 that it would not allow CIA employees to be investigated or prosecuted for such actions. This gutted not just treaty obligations but the Nuremberg principles of international law. When courts in countries such as Spain moved to investigate Bush officials for war crimes, the Obama administration reportedly urged foreign officials not to allow such cases to proceed, despite the fact that the United States has long claimed the same authority with regard to alleged war criminals in other countries. (Various nations have resisted investigations of officials accused of war crimes and torture. Some, such as Serbia and Chile, eventually relented to comply with international law; countries that have denied independent investigations include Iran, Syria and China.)

Secret court

The government has increased its use of the secret Foreign Intelligence Surveillance Court, which has expanded its secret warrants to include individuals deemed to be aiding or abetting hostile foreign governments or organizations. In 2011, Obama renewed these powers, including allowing secret searches of individuals who are not part of an identifiable terrorist group. The administration has asserted the right to ignore congressional limits on such surveillance. (Pakistan places national security surveillance under the unchecked powers of the military or intelligence services.)

Immunity from judicial review

Like the Bush administration, the Obama administration has successfully pushed for immunity for companies that assist in warrantless surveillance of citizens, blocking the ability of citizens to challenge the violation of privacy. (Similarly, China has maintained sweeping immunity claims both inside and outside the country and routinely blocks lawsuits against private companies.)

Continual monitoring of citizens

The Obama administration has successfully defended its claim that it can use GPS devices to monitor every move of targeted citizens without securing any court order or review. (Saudi Arabia has installed massive public surveillance systems, while Cuba is notorious for active monitoring of selected citizens.)

Extraordinary renditions

The government now has the ability to transfer both citizens and noncitizens to another country under a system known as extraordinary rendition, which has been denounced as using other countries, such as Syria, Saudi Arabia, Egypt and Pakistan, to torture suspects. The Obama administration says it is not continuing the abuses of this practice under Bush, but it insists on the unfettered right to order such transfers — including the possible transfer of U.S. citizens.

These new laws have come with an infusion of money into an expanded security system on the state and federal levels, including more public surveillance cameras, tens of thousands of security personnel and a massive expansion of a terrorist-chasing bureaucracy.

Some politicians shrug and say these increased powers are merely a response to the times we live in. Thus, Sen. Lindsey Graham (R-S.C.) could declare in an interview last spring without objection that "free speech is a great idea, but we're in a war." Of course, terrorism will never "surrender" and end this particular "war."

Other politicians rationalize that, while such powers may exist, it really comes down to how they are used. This is a common response by liberals who cannot bring themselves to denounce Obama as they did Bush. Sen. Carl Levin (D-Mich.), for instance, has insisted that Congress is not making any decision on indefinite detention: "That is a decision which we leave where it belongs — in the executive branch."

And in a signing statement with the defense authorization bill, Obama said he does not intend to use the latest power to indefinitely imprison citizens. Yet, he still accepted the power as a sort of regretful autocrat.

An authoritarian nation is defined not just by the use of authoritarian powers, but by the ability to use them. If a president can take away your freedom or your life on his own authority, all rights become little more than a discretionary grant subject to executive will.

The framers lived under autocratic rule and understood this danger better than we do. James Madison famously warned that we needed a system that did not depend on the good intentions or motivations of our rulers: "If men were angels, no government would be necessary."

Benjamin Franklin was more direct. In 1787, a Mrs. Powel confronted Franklin after the signing of the Constitution and asked, "Well, Doctor, what have we got — a republic or a monarchy?" His response was a bit chilling: "A republic, Madam, if you can keep it."

Since 9/11, we have created the very government the framers feared: a government with sweeping and largely unchecked powers resting on the hope that they will be used wisely.

The indefinite-detention provision in the defense authorization bill seemed to many civil libertarians like a betrayal by Obama. While the president had promised to veto the law over that provision, Levin, a sponsor of the bill, disclosed on the Senate floor that it was in fact the White House that approved the removal of any exception for citizens from indefinite detention.

Dishonesty from politicians is nothing new for Americans. The real question is whether we are lying to ourselves when we call this country the land of the free. The ball is in your court, you have the right to judge if truly America is still a free land. But for me, I totally disagree with the word "free land", it should rather be called coward land and home to racism, hate and police brutality.

For America to become that united and great nation it once use to be, then the government must work hard, say the truth about what the nation is facing, work on the mind of every citizen, discourage hate, set a strong law that will not tolerate any racist act, and go ahead to abolish the use of guns by everyone and stop police brutality. It is only then America can reclaim it lost glory and be proud of a better tomorrow.